The Best Fight

a memoir of a martial art practitioner, publisher, and author

by Michael A. DeMarco, M.A.

Disclaimer
Please note that the author and publisher of this book are not responsible in any manner whatsoever for any injury that may result from practicing the techniques and/or following the instructions given herein. Participation in martial arts activities can be dangerous and can lead to serious injury. The material presented in this book is intended for reference only, and the reader assumes all risks associated with attempting to perform any of the activities described herein. Before attempting any of the physical activities described in this book, the reader should consult a physician for advice regarding their individual suitability for performing such activity.

All Rights Reserved
No part of this publication, including illustrations, may be reproduced or utilized in any form or by any means, electronic or mechanical, including photocopying, recording, or by any information storage and retrieval system (beyond that copying permitted by sections 107 and 108 of the US Copyright Law and except by reviewers for the public press), without written permission from Via Media Publishing Company.

Warning: Any unauthorized act in relation to a copyright work may result in both a civil claim for damages and criminal prosecution.

Copyright © 2023
by Via Media Publishing Company
941 Calle Mejia #822, Santa Fe, NM 87501 USA

Book and cover design
by Via Media Publishing Company

Cover illustration
Michael DeMarco practicing along the bosque of the
Rio Grande River in Albuquerque, New Mexico.
Photography by Jose Leon Castillo.

ISBN 978-1-893765-52-8

www.viamediapublishing.com

Dedication

To all those who have participated
in the *Journal of Asian Martial Arts*
and Via Media's book projects
— authors, scholars, practitioners, artists, and readers —

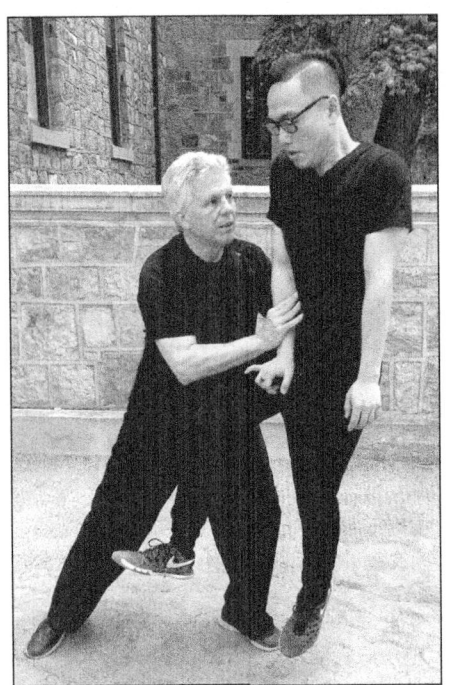

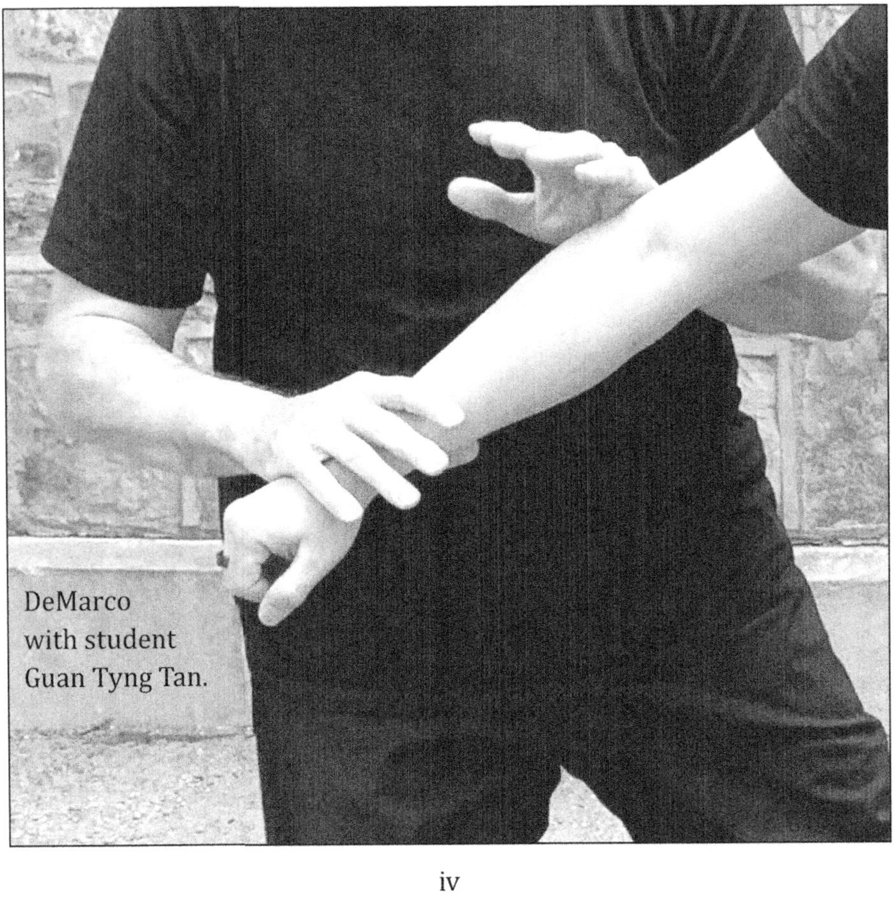

DeMarco with student Guan Tyng Tan.

Table of Contents

Preface — vii

I KUNTAO-SILAT: CHINESE HANDS, INDONESIAN FEET
Martial Essence: Pepperman and Sykes — 1
Five Quarters for a Dollar: Richard Lopez — 8
Count Willem Reeders' Royal Kung Fu — 13
Article: Practical Fighting Strategies of Indonesian Kuntao-Silat in the Willem Reeders Tradition — 21

II YANG AND CHEN TAIJIQUAN: UNIVERSAL PRINCIPLES
Yang Qingyu's Compassionate Presence — 31
Article: Xiong Yanghe's Taiji in Taiwan — 35
A Unicorn Appears: Chen Taiji Stylist Du Yuze — 43
Article: A Brief Description of Chen Style Master Du Yuze — 48

III VIA MEDIA PUBLISHING: PURSUING THE MIDDLE WAY
Tilling the Field of Asian Martial Arts Study — 53
Setting Goals for the *Journal of Asian Martial Arts* — 55
Starting Via Media Publishing Company — 56
Realities of Publishing the *Journal of Asian Martial Arts* — 57
Publishing Pleasures — 61
Finale — 62

IV JOURNAL OF ASIAN MARTIAL ARTS: Contents & Comments — 65

V OTHER VIA MEDIA PUBLICATIONS: Anthologies & Books — 103

VI TRANSFERRING A MARTIAL TRADITION
Teaching and Learning in Erie, PA — 109
Teaching and Learning in Santa Fe, NM — 112
Enter the Novice Student — 114
The Winged Lion School of Tai Chi — 117

Postscript — 121

General Index — 122
Author Index (published in the Journal of Asian Martial Arts) — 127

> The supreme art of war is to subdue the enemy without fighting.
> ~ Sun Tzu

Preface

A needle may draw a thread through printed pages to bind a book. In this little memoir, I feel like a needle that drew a common thread though a segment of martial art history. When I began studying martial arts I didn't know how they would consume my life during the following decades. This book details three interrelated activities: (1) martial art studies, (2) involvement as founder of Via Media Publishing, producing a quarterly journal and books, and (3) experience teaching martial arts.

Publishers, writers, researchers and serious martial art practitioners will benefit with the detailed overview of Via Media and its publications. Via Media produced the *Journal of Asian Martial Arts*, known for its high academic and aesthetic standards. Its contents reflect the history of two decades and provides rich information for practitioners and scholars, making *The Best Fight* a valuable reference work.

In addition to reading, the primary way to learn a martial art is through instruction. In reading about my studies and teaching experience, readers can relate to their own involvement in martial arts. What is important here is the portrayal of my instructors, their teaching methods, and reasons for being involved in martial arts. Their accounts should offer insights and inspiration for others who study and practice any martial art.

At the end of 1991, I founded Via Media Publishing and concurrently started teaching martial arts when the first issue of the *Journal of Asian Martial Arts* came off the press. With the founding of the journal came a leap from the typical mass market periodicals of the time to a scholarly standard. The subject matter in each journal is especially important for researchers. The topics and bibliographies reflect the scholarly work over twenty years by respected authors. High academic and aesthetic standards made the journal unique. Practitioners with exceptional experience also contributed to each journal. In these pages, readers can become familiar with these scholar-practitioners who should be recognized for their contributions to the field of martial arts.

Twenty years later, economics forced an end to the journal. Via Media continued to publish books and began producing anthologies. Chapter Three details the story of Via Media and Chapter Four the story the journal—accounts of special interest to publishers and readers of martial topics. All journal articles are listed by year with some comments, including related matters that ocurred during the same period, such as seminars, conferences, and participation in documentaries. My hope is that others will take the scholarly studies to higher level, ideally with support from universities and other academic institutes. Perhaps future publications can give a better direction for the practice of combatives.

In Chapter Five, an alphabetical list of Via Media anthologies is provided for reference. Each anthology contains material from the *Journal of Asian Martial Arts* organized under common themes, practical for both researchers and practitioners. Also, a list of books published to date shows martial themes as well as an expansion into fiction and historico-political topics.

The final chapter is an account of my years teaching taijiquan. Again, readers should relate to their own experience studying or teaching, regardless of style. All martial art classes are comprised of a variety of characters of different ages, abilities, and temperament. Since the process of learning and teaching goes hand-in-hand, this chapter brings in the importance of how an instructor relates to students. There is a choice teachers have in the curriculum they design for students. Each teacher and school has its own flavor resulting from what they prefer to teach. For example, some schools focus on sport while others may be geared for self-defense or health. By becoming aware of the possibilities, teachers can become better equipped to nurture their students with the blessings of quality martial art instruction.

In this book, students will find a kinship with the stories of progressive learning spanning decades. There certainly are big differences in how and why individuals wish to study a martial art. Their reasons can change over time. Instructors will also find a kinship with the stories of teaching and relate to how their purpose can alter over time. Via Media publications focused on the topic of teaching methodologies and all fascets of Asian martial traditions. May all—students, teachers, and researchers—find useful information in this publication that will enhance their involvement in this fascinating field of study and practice.

• • •

Notes

Chapter I

Kuntao-Silat: Chinese Hands, Indonesian Feet

Martial Essence: Pepperman and Sykes

My introduction to the martial arts was accidental. I can't remember the details as to exactly when and where it happened. I do remember that I was attending Sacred Heart Grade School in Erie, PA, transitioning into eight grade in 1966. The dawn of puberty may have contributed to the foggy memory. At the time, I had some fuzz on my chin and was one of the tallest among classmates. I haven't gotten much taller since. There was some wrestling with the nuns, who would take you by the ear to a bathroom to cut your hair if it was too long. They didn't like my Elvis style, but my dad didn't concur with their wishes. He had the same hair style. I wasn't influenced by Elvis, but nobody could be sheltered from the advent of The Beatles.

Then came weekly guitar lessons. After learning three chords, others appeared having the bright idea that we could actually play music: Jeff Orlando (bass), Sid Michaels (guitar), Luther Gibbs (drums), Eric Johnson (guitar). . . But we needed a singer. Someone volunteered a guy named Thomas Pepperman (1951–2013). As we struggled with three-chord progressions, Tom was a natural singer. He knew the lines and hit the notes effortlessly. He had a bluesy voice, close to a Paul Butterfield or Charlie Musslewhite. Along with the rock-and-roll standards, we did play some blues.

The band practiced at the home of Luther's parents, which wasn't in the better part of town. And Tom lived smack dab in one of the rougher areas. It is no little wonder why Tom was studying a martial art. I wasn't comfortable in his neighborhood even during daylight hours. Many parts of the city were unsafe and I thought it wise to ask Tom if I could also learn self-defense. He took me to meet his teacher, Arthur "Sonny" Sykes (1934–2008). It is only by looking back over the decades that I now see the significance of this as a life-changing event.

Sometimes Sykes stayed in Erie, but he was living in Cleveland at this time. Anytime he came to Erie, we'd workout. I remember the first time going up a couple flights of stairs above a bar in an old building on 6th and French Streets to a studio. Others taught in the space on that floor too, but we'd be there when others were not around. A large painted dragon decorated a wall. The old wooden floors had been sanded smooth and painted grey. Dressing rooms were in the back. Large windows faced the two-block area called Perry Square, named after Admiral Matthew Perry, famed naval commander during the Battle of 1812 on Lake Erie. Perry's name may be familiar to some for his role in the 1854 Convention of Kanagawa which opened Japan to the West.

Over the months, it was usually only Sykes, Tom and myself meeting together to work out. Sykes would show us techniques. Tom and I would repeat and repeat a new single technique for hours and regularly review over following months. He was more advanced than his brown belt indicated. Working with him certainly nurtured my practice. Often I'd work on individual techniques while he practiced a solo barehanded routine or with weapons. We varied our practices according to Sykes guidance. Many days just Tom and I worked out, reviewing lessons and sparring.

The techniques Sykes was teaching focused on evasive shifting and stepping in unison with various combinations of blocking, deflecting, and striking. We'd move according to imaginary geometric patterns on the floor based on a triangle, usually standing on one point and moving to the other two, or standing on two points and stepping to the third. One triangle could be attached to another, so the foot patterns could get complex. With enough triangles, circles could be formed. In normal practice, we didn't think much about this. We just moved.

Of course stepping patterns worked in tandem with the whole body to perform any strike, kick, reap, throw, or break. Mainly closed-hand techniques would be used in tournaments, but much of the system called for open-hand techniques useful for grabs, strikes to the most vulnerable areas (eyes, throat and groin), and to vital points. Hand formations became tools, for example: a claw shape suitable to grasp an opponent's jawbone, a single knuckle that fits into the jugular notch, or using the index finger for eye strikes while the other fingers serve to prevent too deep a penetration by coming against the cheekbone. Each movement was executed for maximum effect. Rather than simply block an incoming punch, a block/strike could be utilized to break the elbow. Rather than sweep a leg, the knee was destroyed. Sykes' teacher, Willem Reeders, was quoted as saying: "We are dirty fighters." Many of the individual techniques were embodied in solo routines. Training always alloted time for sparring.

Later, I discovered that this wasn't how other martial art instructors taught. They usually had schools occupied with a dozen or more students. The only reason why we practiced this way—basically private lessons—was because Tom was like an adopted son for Sykes. Sykes had dated Tom's mother and they remained good friends. Affection would show in small ways, Sykes always called him "Tommy," even though Tom was a few years older than I and a senior attending Academy High School. Little Tommy had grown up.

I can't remember when the building on French Street was torn down and became the location of Erie Insurance Corporate Headquarters. We moved over to another old building called Pythian Temple at 524 West 17th Street. This was once a building for the fraternal organization known as The Knights of Pythias. For us, the second floor served well for our practice with a huge area. Its wooden floor was maintained well, since we always sparred barefoot. I remember seeing it darken by spots of sweat from our workouts. At this location, new students joined and classes became larger. More students for practicing techniques in pairs and for sparring.

The new students presented different characters. Most were good classmates, but sometimes there would be a troublemaker. Now with the larger classes, there was much activity. I was working individual techniques while a few others were sparring. One big guy who was sparring started yelling at his opponent in a blood rage. Sykes quickly moved toward them and, speaking is a soft voice, cooled down the heated conflict. He managed to keep a wonderful atmosphere in classes, with an emphasis on respect. Rarely would anyone get hurt, even during the most intense sparring sessions, in large part because control and accuracy were emphasized for any and every technique.

When I was promoted from white belt to green, Tom gifted a belt to me which was originally give to him by Sykes, and to Sykes from his teacher, Willem Reeders. I didn't think much about belts. I was just happy learning and enjoying our friendships. Tom was promoted to orange sash, and was fighting in the black belt category at tournaments. I spent much time with Tom in and out of the *dojo* — a Japanese term most Americans used for the practice hall. Many called our art "karate," but we knew it as Royal Kung Fu.* It took me a few more years to comprehend the full significance of the name.

* *The romanization for "kung fu" is now usually spelled as "gongfu." Reeders called his school Royal Kung Fu, which will be used in this book with reference to his school. Gongfu will be used in other cases when referring to Chinese martial arts.*

Arthur Sykes about to break seven cement slabs. Courtesy of T. Pepperman.

The art took time to learn as did the history and who was involved in its development and transmission. The main figure was Grandmaster Willem Reeders, who I was told was of royal Chinese and Dutch heritage. He came to the USA from Indonesia. I met him and many of his senior students, including Richard Lopez, Raymond Cunningham, Guy Savelli, Patrick Sheldon, and others. During my high school years, I'd go to tournaments in Pennsylvania and neighboring states, representing Sykes' school. Many other teachers and styles would be present, mainly Okinawan karate stylists.

In the late 1960s and early 1970s, most Americans were only familiar with karate and judo. The "little dragon," Bruce Lee, had not yet entered the scene. Tournament judges favored there own styles, so it wasn't easy to win trophies if you were a Royal Kung Fu practitioner. The judges didn't understand our techniques, which often appeared softer than karate. For example, a karate practitioner would strongly block a kick at their head, fiercely pushing the attacking foot far off line. For the same type of attack, we'd shift away and deflect with one hand brought up near the ear. The kicking foot may be close to our head, but it was as good as a mile away. There is no need to over-extend such a block, which then offers an additional target for your opponent. It took many more years for judges

Thomas Pepperman. Arthur "Sonny" Sykes.

to learn about the logic of Chinese styles and how they worked.

Besides the bias of style, Sykes was a black man, a very black one! There was prejudice against him and his students because of this. He was also an extremely good martial artist and jealousy filled the room when he'd walk into a tournament. Once I was sitting in the bleachers waiting for a tournament to begin. Schools were arriving by busloads. One well known high-ranking instructor stopped in front of me to ask another instructor: "Is Sykes here?" If Sykes was present and entered in the tournament, experienced black belts knew they would have a very difficult fight for a first place trophy.

Those entering tournaments could participant in different categories, usually being forms, sparring, and breaking. For forms, each performer would announce their personal name, style, school, and the name of the routine they intended to demonstrate. I've seen Sykes enter the black belt division doing forms I never saw previously. He could jump into the air with a silken sidekick that struck out and returned like lightning. Accurate to their targets, his hand strikes were blurs of color. If there was a tie for first place, the referees would ask the two participants to perform again. Sykes would usually announce the name of a different form to perform. Later I learned he just spontaneously improvised forms. It is difficult

Michael DeMarco, Tom Pepperman, Jeff Orlando & David Lewis.

enough to practice a form thousands of times and later perform it well in front of judges. Although he did memorize and teach many routines, Sykes could create a form on the spot. It'd be flawless. Try to move through a few seconds of improvised techniques at fighting speed and discover the difficulty. To this day, I don't know anyone else who can do this.

Sykes and Tom always did well in the fighting division. What was fascinating to me was that most of what we practiced in the studio could not be used in tournament fighting. Trophies were won with points. The Reeders system was for real fighting, not competition. The techniques were to cripple or maim, so we limited and adapted for tournaments.

Sykes was caring for all his students. At tournaments, he'd closely watch the fighting bouts for fairness and safety. I never saw him angry. He'd face problems calmly as he would while competing on the floor. During the years I studied with him, he treated me as family, with kindness, patience, and understanding. The first time he gave me a ride to my parents he met my father. "Hey Dad! Look who I brought home!" It was a rare occurence to see a white man and a charcoal-black man greet and shake hands in a middle-class milky neighborhood during the early 70s, the time following the Watts riots in Los Angeles. This is a great memory for me because the two men were similar in many ways. A bow for their ability to have sympathy for everyone.

My father, Ralph DeMarco, never studied martial arts, although he was a superb athlete in many sports. Tom was at my parents home one day and we were talking about breaking methods. Tom showed me how to break a red brick. Not any easy feat. If attempted with poor technique, it is an excellent way to break one's finger bones or wrist. My father watched us, walked over, kneeled down, and broke a brick on his first try. I'm glad my dad never spanked me during my youth.

As mentioned, I had some difficult classmates, and Sykes did too. At the start of our workout at the Pythian Temple on a particular day, one of Reeders' students came in wearing a red sash. Standing in the middle of the big room, he challenged Sykes. Our teacher walked slowly out from the dressing room and sat on a chair facing the floor. Why was the challenge made? I am unsure of all the details, but it seems there was a question of the authenticity of the high rank shown by the red sash. Sykes didn't go on the floor, but softly spoke until the unwelcomed guest left, the intruder promising to the settle the matter at another time and place. Looking back on this strange episode, it is clear that Sykes did not accept the challenge because he knew the only end would be with someone severely wounded or perhaps even in a death. He didn't need to prove anything in that way.

Months later, Tom and I went to meet Sykes at the Pythian Temple to practice. It was out of the ordinary that about a dozen black belt holders were also arriving. Sykes arranged a few long tables for them to sit and talk in the side room while Tom and I practiced in the main room. The meeting was to discuss what they could do about this challenger. How to prove he did nor did not deserve and receive a red sash? The black belts were of various styles and the question of rank was difficult for them to solve in this particular case. Their meeting had no results.

By the early 1970s, Sykes was unable to come to Erie so often. Tom and I looked for a school, mainly for practice space. We went to a few schools, including Vincent Christiano's and Gerald Durante's Goshin Jutsu karate dojos. Christiano was a good fighter. One of his favored techniques was to jump high into the air to come down upon you with an overhead strike (*shuto*). It was 95% successful because he was a large man, falling on you like a tidal wave. The shuto was only the coup de grâce. We also attended Durate's classes. I enjoyed working with one of his top black belt students and gentleman, Steve Capella. Durate registered me in Japan as a purple belt. But, Tom and I were already infused with Royal Kung Fu and we didn't stay very long at the school.

At one tournament, off to the side, Durante was demonstrating with Japanese *sai* (a short metal weapon with two prongs; see page 14 photograph) techniques to Reeders and others. Reeders was watching, standing motionless in his typical mode, with his arms hanging down, hands crossed in front. As the sais glistened through the air flipping and spinning, Reeders suddenly plucked both sais away with one hand while they were in movement. Reeders style was not so flashy. All his techniques—open hand and with weapons—focused on the practical. Tom was becoming quite familiar using the sais and knives. I hadn't started any weapons work as yet.

Tom opened his own school on Eleventh and State Streets. At least a few hundred people attended the grand opening. Tom was getting many students, no doubt in large part due to Bruce Lee's raising star. Much changed. I loved Royal Kung Fu, but didn't want to spend time with some of the new students. As with Reeders' following and Sykes' following, Tom was getting some problem students. In order to keep a distance from those I felt were of low character, I decided to sacrifice studies. I didn't know if I would ever study with anyone else again.

Five Quarters for a Dollar: Richard Lopez

Some months passed. I went to a car wash and needed four quarters for a dollar to start the machine. I asked a guy in the next stall if he had

Richard Lopez at left with the author.

change. He said he recognized me from the black belt meeting at the Pythian Temple. His name was Richard Lopez (1933–2014), another student of Willem Reeders. After learning that I stopped studying under Sykes and Pepperman, he invited me to where he was teaching. It was in a studio behind the home of another Willem Reeders student named Raymond Cunningham (1928–2008), located at 439 East 6th Street. Ray was a tough ex-Marine with good, often salty, humor. He had a nice small studio behind his house. Although Cunningham, Sykes, and Lopez had the same teacher, there were differences in how they moved individually. Both Cunningham and Lopez utilized more tension in their movement than Sykes, but they had an excellent repertoire of techniques and knew how to use them. Both had studied karate previously which probably influenced their gongfu. Cunningham's skills were tested on his job. He worked twenty-six years as a detective for Norfolk and Southern Railroad where he thwarted a number of would-be train robberies.

The 6th Street studio remains vivid in my mind. In the winter, I'd arrive early to shovel a path through the snow down the long driveway leading to it. There was a small office on the left of the entry with a smaller bathroom/dressing room. The workout area was not large. Only two people could spar at a time. Two photos of Reeders were on one wall, and one of judo founder Jigoro Kano. At center was set of *taichu* (jp. *sai*) mounted in a triangular shaped board. Judo matts were rolled up and kept along the same wall. A long closet contained a number of judo uniforms. Only eight to a dozen students were in a class, usually only working techniques in pairs. No real sparring. We did practice some throws and falls. A benefit was that Lopez did start me with basic weapons practice: taichu, knives, staff, and broadsword.

Lopez loved working with weapons and actually made many. He made personalized sets of taichu for Reeders according to specifications Reeders set down. I've held a heavy set made for practice, seemingly designed for weightlifters. Of course others made for regular usage would then seem relatively light. Even the regular sais were substantial, making the store-bought models feel like toys. In Japanese, *sai* (釵) means "hair pin" because of its shape. It is called "iron ruler" (*tie chi* 鐵尺) in Chinese, *tekpi* in Malay; *chabang* or *tjabang* in Indonesian, and *tepi* in the Hokkien language that Reeders spoke. Reeders usually called them "iron ruler" or *taichu* in Hokkien. Reeders explained to Lopez that the taichu's length should properly match the length of the practitioner's forearm. The distance between the main section and the prongs were measured by finger-widths so as not to be too tight or too loose for maneuvering.

Time moved on. While living twenty miles away on the campus of Edinboro University (now called PennWest), I'd get to Lopez's class once a week. Some of the usual practitioners there included Mark Anthony, Joe Sanfratello, Ron Cargioli, Peter Pjecha, and Jerry Hayes. Good memories of the studio and also the after-class shrimp and a beer at the Friendly's Tavern on West 8th and Chestnut Street.

When Lopez purchased a house at 1012 West 27th Street, he converted a two-car garage behind the home to include a second floor studio. Some students continued at this location and new students joined classes, including Charles Page, Tony Flagella, Michael Marchini, Ed Brooks, and Al Mele. A few helped in the studio's construction. I painted a four-by-eight foot dragon for the wall. Unlike regular dragon designs, this one had five talons, a symbol of royalty. Other instructors would sometime visit the Lopez studio, especially local karateka such as Billy Blanks, Ralph Porfilio, and Artis Simmons.

While home from college for the weekend, Lopez called to invite me out for a for Chinese dinner at the Inn of Double Happiness on Peach and Liberty Streets. When I arrived at the restaurant, he was sitting at a big table with his wife Alice and a few others. It was on this night that he presented me with an orange sash—equivalent to a black belt. I was his only orange sash. I appreciated it, but I never wore it. Thinking of all the familiar schools, I had seen so many undeserved black belts that I questioned the real value of rank. Plus there were others of great talent who weren't promoted. Lopez would periodically tell me to wear the belt. Eventually he gave up talking about it. Even later, he stopped wearing his third-degree orange sash. Knowledge was more important than the belt. However, forty years later I told Lopez I should have wore it just because it was from him.

The author with Master Lopez at the 27th Street studio (May1998)
and below on West 6th Street (cir. 1975).

Richard Lopez demonstrating with taichus. 6th St. studio.

As part of my undergraduate work, I went to study philosophy in India in 1974 at Vivekananda College, affiliated with the University of Madras. That brought an end to my regular studies with Lopez. However we remained in close touch for the next forty years. He became like a father and we met often as close friends.

Considering the length of time studying at the 6th Street and 27th Street studios, I didn't make much progress in martial skill. I would eventually go to Taiwan to study. At that time Lopez said he didn't have anything more to teach me. He had years of experience in judo, karate, and the Reeders system. He had more cards up his sleeve, but didn't feel they would add to my deck. What he shared were personal stories of his martial art studies, including his knowledge of Willem Reeders and the Royal Kung Fu system.

During those more than forty years with Lopez, he shared much with me. I learned it was he who found and remodeled the studio on 6th and French. He talked of the tournaments and all of Reeders students. He often talked with great respect about Robert Servidio, who he eventually introduced to me. Servidio is perhaps the most knowledgable about Reeders' system. Like the Grandmaster, Servidio has a triad on his hand, three small dots tattooed on his purlicue—the space between the thumb and the forefinger. The dots have a special significance for Reeders and the martial system.

Count Willem Reeders' Royal Kung Fu

Lopez had studied karate and judo. He held a black belt rank in judo before he went into the military. Stationed in Germany, he enjoyed regular practice there with excellent judoka. After returning to the USA, he heard of a great judo master teaching in the Jamestown-Dunkirk area in New York state. Like meeting ET, this was the first contact with Master Reeders. After a hands-on minute, Lopez knew Reeders' skill was way beyond any other judo instructors he met in the US or Germany. Only later did he learn that Reeders primary martial art was Royal Kung Fu.

Of course Lopez spread the word in the Erie area about his new judo teacher and others began taking the hour's drive to Dunkirk to study. Eventually, the judo and karate practitioners switched to gongfu. Workouts with Reeders changed their perception of martial arts. This was not tournament play. Sparring was at a level unseen until arriving at the Dunkirk studio. Lopez said he'd often return home and immediately opened the kitchen refrigerator and put his hands inside the freezer. Sometimes his head too. Reeders left traces of the workout on the bodies of those he sparred. Each student got toughened in the process . . . or left.

Reeders had close ties to martial art groups in Toronto, Canada. Lopez drove Reeders there to meet Sam Wong at his Mu Dong Martial Arts School. In Mandarin, *Mu Dong* is romanized as *Wu Dong* (武當) a famous Daoist mountain area in the northwestern part of Hubei Province, China. Grandmaster Wong and Grandmaster Reeders became good friends and together founded the Chinese Gongfu Federation (*Chunghwa Kung Fu Hui*). When arriving at Wong's school, Reeders walked in like royalty, but Lopez was not allowed in. He was caucasian. Specialized instruction was reserved for those who met the proper cultural criteria. This is an example of the attitude of the time found in many Chinese gongfu schools in Western countries and in Asia.

From Lopez and others, my ears became filled with stories about Master Reeders and the Royal Kung Fu system. Over the decades, the stories multiplied and transformed. There were many things that obscured the truth. Reeders did not speak English very well. Japanese terminology was usually used to describe the system. Americans didn't understand the full significance of Japanese terms and zilch of the even less familiar Hokkien/Chinese. Compound this with exaggerations and outright lies, the blurry image of Grandmaster Reeders faded more over the years as does an old sepia photo.

One highly respected Reeders student gave a lecture with hundreds in attendance. He said that gongfu (*kungfu*) as a martial art traces back

Willem Andreas Reeders in Albuquerque, NM. Courtesy of Robert Servideo.

to Confucius. The sage's name is often romanized as Kong Fu-zi, which seems like a variant spelling of kungfu. He was from the Kong clan. *Zi* signifies master. Impressive research with a faulty conclusion. The Chinese characters referring to the sage (孔夫) and martial arts (功夫) are different. There is no connection in meaning.

Often there is confusion in martial terminology and the various romanization systems used resulting in different spellings for the same Chinese words. There is *quanfa* (*chuanfa*; 拳法): *quan* meaning "boxing or fist" and *fa* meaning "law, way or method." *Gongfu* (*kungfu*; 功夫) can simply translate as "effort" to gain skill (not only martial skill). Then we come to the term *kuntao*, which is the term denoting the Chinese martial arts of the Chinese communities in Southeast Asia. It's spelled as *kuntaw* in the Tagalog language of the Philippines. Although there isn't an exact Chinese rendition, the characters *quandao* (boxing way/methods) are most often used as an equivalent. None of these terms—quanfa, gongfu, quandao, or kuntao—are styles.

Since Willem Reeders lived in Indonesia, he learned some indigenous martial arts found in the Indonesian Archipelago known as *silat*. Like the terms mentioned above, silat is not a style. There are hundreds of different silat styles. Reeders came to call his art Royal Kung Fu because his gongfu was associated with his family style, and his family were of royal lineage. Some articles show this status when referring to "Count Willem Reeders."

Reeders in Indonesia

Willem Andreas Reeders was born on October 29, 1917, in Surabaya, East Java, Indonesia. He passed on August 14, 1990, in Albuquerque, New Mexico. For over 72 years his life was infused by martial arts. His life's story is colorful. I present facts regarding his family and martial arts, and add some of the stories that also may ring true. Researching his family showed many Ancestry.com records are "private." Records in Indonesia are difficult to find. Many of the people listed where married a second time. A contributing factor to the difficulty in tracing family lineages is that the Japanese invaded of the Dutch East Indies in 1942, overrunning the entire colony in less than three months.

Willem's father, Cornelis Marinis Reeders (1881-1945) was born in the village of Poortvliet, in the province of Veeland, Netherlands. This is about 35 miles north of Antwerp. Some references note that his mother was Christina Wieling (1910-1997) born in Wier, in north-west Netherlands. However, this doesn't seem correct. She was only seven years old when Willem was born. Perhaps she was his stepmother. Later, in 1936, she married Jippe De Vries.

We do know that Willem and his brother Theo Cornelis Reeders (1920-1945) were born in Surabaya, Indonesia. They lived on a tea plantation operated by the Wieling Family. The Reeders and Wieling families no doubt bonded through marriages. They were well to do business people who provided for their children. Their status reflected royalty. Oral tradition states that one of the relatives, Karel Lodewijk, represented a branch of Dutch royalty, sent on a diplomatic mission to China in order to establish formal tea trade agreements. Or course, his social status would be met with like status in China. He met Princess Hap Kiem (Chiem 詹?) and they wanted to marry. However, there was strong resistance. Karl and the Princess found a solution with the help of her brother, Liu Seong. Using his influence, Liu Seong made the necessary arrangements and the couple secretly moved to the Indonesian island of Java and created the family plantation in East Java. Notes show that Princess Hap Kiem was from a city named Haiko (海口?) which seems to be the capitol of the island province of Hainan, China. This is the only city with that pronunciation I found in south China where people speak Hokkien, the native language spoken in the Reeders family.

Ernest DeVries, Liu Siong, and Willem Reeders. Courtesy of R. Lopez.

Princess Hap Kiem's brother, Liu Seong, was said to be the bearer of the royal family's martial art tradition. As a family tradition, his boxing style no doubt carried some unique characteristics, but would certainly evolve over the next generation. Liu Seong brought his twelve-year-old nephew to the Shaolin Temple in the early 1930's in order to study martial arts, medicine, and other topics. They did an annual one-hundred day intensive there every year for ten years.

Young Willem fought often as a youth, sometimes in childhood brawls, and other times in organized fight matches. His older sister, Adriana Engelina Reeders, would repair his torn clothings after his fights. One huge tournament was organized with fighters coming from near and far. The winner was Willem Reeders, who was presented with a pair of golden taichu. The weapons later becoming a symbol on his school's patch.

Willem's combat expertise helped when he served in the Royal Dutch Indonesian Army and also during the Indonesian fight for independence. He carried out sabotage missions against the Japanese under the code name "Red Ant," later to be a title of an article about his exploits as covered decades later in *Action for Men* magazine. He was captured by the Japanese, but escaped.

Reeders and his Uncle in Indonesia. Photos courtesy of R. Lopez.

When Willem was a prisoner of war in Nakhom Pathom, a city in central Thailand, he met Ernest "Nes" De Vries. De Vries had studied Pukulan with Mas Djut, bodyguard to the Sultan of Pontianak on Borneo. The two became good friends and shared their martial knowledge. De Vries introduced his nephews to Reeders, the de Thouars brothers: William, Paul, Maurice, and Victor. Other Reeders family members were prisoners of war. Willem's father Cornelis and his brother Theo were at the Ambarawa internment camp. Both died on June 3, 1945, no doubt by the hands of the Japanese invaders. Cornelis is buried at Ereveld Kalibanteng (Dutch War Cemetery), in Semarang, Central Java, Indonesia.

Ray Cunningham (l.) and Robert Servideo attacking Reeders. Courtesy of R. Lopez.

After the war, Willem went to Holland. Once there, he immediately, applied for a visa to the United States. He spent time in New York. In the late 1950s he moved to Toronto, Canada, then to Dunkirk, NY. While in Dunkirk, he started teaching in Erie, PA, in 1962, at Raymond Cunningham's studio. In 1972, he finally settled in Albuquerque, New Mexico. Wherever he went, people sought him out. Apparently even Hollywood knocked on his door. It's said that Bruce Lee noted in letters that he met with Reeders. If this is true, probably Danny Innosanto made the introduction, since he worked in the film industry and was a silat practitioner. The TV program *Kung Fu* starring David Carradine may have gotten elements for the main plot from Reeders, such as the blind teacher and Carradine's moving to the West.

While studying with Art Sykes, I met Reeders a few times at tournaments. The last time we met, he came from Albuquerque to visit in Dunkirk, New York. Although it was only a short visit, he wanted to see Richard Lopez, who invited me to go along. We drove to Dunkirk from Erie. At first sight, they approached each other in fighting stances and wide grins. The chance for decades-old-friends to see each other again was a joy to witness. The martial arts was their main bond.

What martial art did Willem Reeders practice and teach? Many have

On the beach of Lake Erie Peninsula, Pennsylvania. Courtesy of R. Lopez.

guessed and jumped to faulty conclusions. Was his great uncle Liu Seong a Shaolin monk, or just a visitor to the temple? He certainly was Willem's main teacher. Willem felt a special dedication to him, especially after his uncle became blind. This catastrophe occurred when a few approached Liu Seong, supposedly to ask for a match to light a cigarette, then threw powered glass into his eyes. The assailants were killed immediately on the spot. Liu Seong went into seclusion, training his nephew Willem until he was ready to represent the family art.

Some say Reeders also studied with a number of silat masters, learned many other styles, including karate, judo, Tibetan Taichi, and baguazhang. Baguazhang? I doubt it. Bagua is a relatively new art from northern China and it was highly unlikely that any representative would be living in the south. Tibetan Taichi? This certainly isn't associated with any form of taijiquan that originated in the Chen Village in Henan Province. Most likely, Reeders called it "tai chi" simply in reference to an exercise form. And all the silat systems? How much time would be needed to study these systems? The conclusions many have jumped to, wishing that Reeders could have absorbed all they say, is unrealistic. There is a better, rational explanation for the vast repertoire of martial skills Reeders possessed.

Reeders lived and studied with Liu Seong. He spent valuable time with Ernest De Vries. So, he no doubt had a great foundation in his Chinese family system, the arts taught at the Shaolin Temple, and Pukulan. He encountered many other masters, most for a relatively short time. For example, he met Dutchman Anton Geesink, a 10th-dan judoka, in the Netherlands. He met Sam Wong in Toronto. Reeders had enough background and, being extraordinarily gifted, could grasp any martial style by its essence. Some say he mastered 81 weapons. Why stop there? Were knife, fork, and chopsticks included in that list? When one has grasped the essence of a universal martial art, all arts become one.

Group photograph at a tournament hosted Arthur Sykes and Richard Lopez, at St. Joseph's Church auditorium, Erie, PA, 1963: Arthur E. Sykes, Gerard Durant (1923-1991), a Canadian instructor, Reeders, and Richard Lopez. Courtesy of R. Lopez. Below: The author with Willem Reeders during his visit to Dunkirk, NY, cir. 1976.

Article adapted from the *Journal of Asian Martial Arts*, Vol. 19 No. 3
Practical Fighting Strategies of Indonesian Kuntao-Silat in the Willem Reeders Tradition

Introduction

What fighting arts are found in Indonesia? Do they have distinguishing traits that we can recognize as unique to that geographic area? Since the Republic of Indonesia is a country that comprises 17,508 islands and is home to over 230 million people, we can be certain there are numerous styles to bewilder any researcher. However, when looking at the variety of Asian martial art styles, there are a few characteristics that may help us distinguish which are Indonesian. Helpful guidelines can be derived from historical and geographical perspectives as well as combative body postures that seem to have been molded by centuries of social norms.

The following pages offer a very brief look at Indonesia's historical development and general features that may have contributed to its unique repertoire of martial art styles. The present understanding among the average reader is limited by the lack of publications about Indonesian martial arts, as well as the scarceness of qualified teachers living outside Indonesia. One important pioneer in bringing Indonesian martial arts to the United States was Willem Andreas Reeders (1917–1990). This short article is a very humble attempt to present aspects of "Bill" Reeders's teachings as indicators of the general state of Indonesian martial arts, how and why they are taught, and the general curricula.

Historical Elements in Indonesian Martial Arts

The world's fourth-most-populous country is blessed with abundant natural resources and has been a center of international trade for over two thousand years. Many ethnic groups came into contact with varying degrees of social mixing. Immigrants from India and China made major cultural contributions to Indonesia. For example, Buddhism and Hinduism mixed with native animism (Wilson, 1993). Muslims from India brought their religion also. Today the country is home to the largest Muslim population in the world. Many immigrants came to work and a large number became leading merchants. Of course, those with financial power played a growing part in the area's local and regional politics.

Europeans were drawn to Indonesia for the spice trade during their "Age of Discovery." The Portuguese were first, arriving in 1512, and the British and Dutch soon followed. The Dutch came to dominate much of the area now known as Indonesia from 1603 to 1949. It wasn't until World War II that circumstances ended Dutch rule. Since Japan invaded and occupied Indonesian islands during the war, and The Netherlands had to focus its energies on postwar rebuilding at home, the resulting strains forced the Dutch to eventually recognize Indonesian independence.

The brief overview presented above indicates the complex nature of Indonesian society. In all, there are over 300 ethnic groups in Indonesia that have contributed to a multicolored cultural tapestry. The resulting fabric possesses a mesmerizing beauty, but also includes inherent tensions stemming from social diversity among the numerous ethnic, cultural, and linguistic groups. Warfare and social disturbances have occurred across the lengthy archipelago in different times and locations over the centuries. Within each social layer the presence of martial arts can be found.

Research on Kuntao-Silat

Cimande, Pencak Silat, Bakti Negara, Cikalong, Harimau, Serak... a long list of terms can describe Indonesian martial art styles. Some styles were named after particular masters, animals, locations, or associated combat terms. Major styles have branches, and branches have offshoots. The easiest way to classify Indonesian martial arts is to demarcate them into the two main categories: (1) *silat*: the indigenous martial arts, and (2) *kuntao* (Mandarin, *quandao*; "fist/boxing ways"): styles of Chinese origin.

Immigrants from China came to Indonesia over many centuries. Some Chinese fled to Southeast Asia as northern Chinese dynasties brought their power into southern China. Others came for work opportunities, and many became leading businessmen and traders. The waves of immigrants included boxing masters, a number of whom were enticed by wealthy merchants to teach Chinese and help protect their business establishments. There are still strong social ties among Chinese-Indonesians; however, social relations between them and native Indonesians remain strained to this day.

Kuntao styles bear resemblance to a number of styles from the Chinese mainland, especially those from the south, such as Shaolin styles of White Crane, Five Animals, etc. Time has allowed Chinese and native Indonesians to build better relationships—through friendships, intermarriages, and business relationships. In turn, this affected the martial arts' development with pure Chinese styles mixing in varying degrees with native Indonesian styles.

Native Indonesians also had a longstanding need to protect their interests, and martial arts permeated their culture from the village level up. Their styles are greatly influenced by ancient animistic beliefs and practices, along with complementary Hindu and Arab beliefs and practices (Wilson, 1993; Farrer, 2009). The resulting cultural blending can be seen in the number of physical arts, especially in dance and theater (Pauka, 1986, 1998, 1999, 2003).

Many combative postures are low to the ground, in part because it is likely that combat would take place on slippery terrain. Indonesia is situated along the equator and is nearly all tropical with long monsoon seasons. Fighting on slippery terrain would necessitate that combatives styles include practical postures allowing one to fight on the ground, as well as provide a flowing continuity between ground and standing postures and vice versa (Davies, 2000). Low postures and ground fighting skills are also practical elements in kuntao-silat's fighting strategy.

Regarding Indonesian martial arts as an academic subject, books and articles of scholarly quality have been sorely lacking, especially compared with martial traditions of China, Japan, and Korea. Indonesian fighting arts have been secretive for centuries, and only in recent decades have there been substantial recordings made on film, in print, and in digital formats. In the early 1970s, Draeger, Alexander, and Chambers presented a glimpse into the martial arts of the archipelago through their books in English. However, no doubt because of the Dutch period of colonization, some of the best writings on kuntao-silat have been published by Europeans who have studied and lived in Indonesia. For example, Dr. Hiltrud Cordes wrote her doctorate dissertation (1990) on Pencak silat. Dr. Kirstin Pauka's dissertation (1999) on Randai theatre was published in CD-ROM format, and she was responsible for the U.S. debut of silat-based Randai theater of West Sumatra (2003). A recent example is Dr. Douglas Farrer's scholarly work dealing with the Muslim Sufi mysticism and silat (2009).

Of course, there is a growing amount of writings on websites about kuntao-silat, but most of it is presented for promotional reasons and is lacking in objectivity and accuracy. Oftentimes materials presented take the reader further from the truth than closer to it!

Migration and the Spread of Kuntao-Silat

There is a large number of martial art practitioners spread throughout the Indonesian archipelago. A relative number are highly skilled, but their names may not be well-known outside their own locale. For fame and honor, there were formerly regular challenge matches, often including weapons. Some masters have gained reputations much like gunfighters in the American "Wild West." Over the centuries, fighting traditions were passed from generation to generation, usually within a family lineage or within a clan. Such arts continue to prosper today under similar conditions, while others are taking the modern route of commercializing kuntao-silat, bringing a few masters international acclaim.

Recent decades have seen a growth of kuntao-silat schools and associations in Indonesia. Ties established during the colonial period between the Netherlands and Indonesia contributed to the introduction and slow-growing presence of kuntao-silat in the Netherlands, where it later was spread into neighboring countries. However, by the mid-20th century, it was still very rare to see any martial art style from Indonesia performed publically outside the archipelago. Writings on Indonesian styles were rare. What could be better to gain knowledge of kuntao-silat than seeing a master in action? Some practitioners began presenting their arts to the public, and taking on students.

A few Dutch-Chinese kuntao-silat practitioners from Java emigrated to the United States in the late 1950s and early 1960s, including Willem Reeders (1917–1990); three brothers, Paul de Thouars (1930–1972), Willem de Thouars (b. 1936), and Victor de Thouars; and Willy Wetzel (1921–1975). Their teachings and presentations brought some recognition of kuntao-silat to people in the United States and Canada.

Willem Reeders's Early Teachings in Western New York

The following pages focus on the teachings of Willem A. Reeders (1917–1990). He moved to the Jamestown, New York, area in the mid-1960s and to Albuquerque, New Mexico, in 1972, where he opened the doors to many new students. In the 1960s most people in the United States were aware of karate and judo, but little else of Asian martial traditions. Stylistically, Reeders's system was a stunning contrast to the karate styles popular during that period. An objective for this article is to look at Reeders's teaching and practice in order to gain one perspective on Indonesian fighting arts that may offer some insight into kuntao-silat systems in general.

Reeders's teachings attracted a number of students from the Jamestown area at the far western corner of New York state. Jerry Bradigan was a longtime student who carries on Reeders's tradition in Fredonia, New York. Marilyn Feeney carries on his teaching in Albuquerque. Others studied with Reeders in Jamestown and also in Erie, Pennsylvania. Noted first-generation students from the Erie area include Raymond Cunningham (1928–2008), Arthur E. Sykes (1934–2008), Richard Lopez (b. 1933-2014), Harry Zimmerman, Ed "Tiny" Sealy, Ed Carter, and Robert Servidio. One of the most respected of Reeders's students is Mr. Servidio, noted for his highly advanced level in the system, as well as his upright character.

What did Reeders teach? Ask his longtime students and their answers vary. According to Reeders's students, his main influence came from his grandmother's brother, Liu Seong, who moved to Indonesia from China. Uncle Liu taught young Willem the family gongfu system. In addition, Reeders studied a number of kuntao and silat styles, plus Shotokan karate and Kodokan judo. From his rich trove of combat skills, he taught different techniques to different students, and changed curricula over time and locations.

Because many were familiar with Japanese martial art terminology, Reeders and students often mixed Japanese terms with unfamiliar Indonesian and Chinese terminology. Many students, unaware of Asian history and language, misinterpreted much. Intentionally or unintentionally, Reeders himself was responsible for passing on inaccuracies regarding the history of what he taught and where his techniques originated. To this day, second- and third-generation practitioners often repeat hearsay as fact, many times adding their own embellishments. Others note the inconsistencies, mistranslations of foreign terms, and hyperbole, and simply state that they cannot clearly separate fact from fiction.

What proves certain is that Willem Reeders taught a variety of styles. As a Dutch-Chinese living in Indonesia, his studies were primarily Chinese-based kuntao styles, but included training in native Indonesian silat styles as well. From his technical repertoire, he taught whatever he wanted. Students may not have known what style they were studying; all they knew was that Reeders was a superb fighter with something special to teach.

First-Generation Representatives: Arthur Sykes and Richard Lopez

In 1965 my introduction to the martial arts came through Arthur

"Sonny" Sykes. My friend and classmate at the time was Thomas Pepperman, one of Sykes's most senior students. I worked out with Tom regularly for a few years. Classes with Mr. Sykes were never regular, but they were always insightful. This period was important for me because it brought a reality of what combatives were designed to do. Performed at a high level of skill, kuntao-silat is fluid, yet powerful and devastating. Practice was sweaty, interesting, and fun. I appreciated the gesture when Tom presented me a green belt, which was originally given to him by Sykes. Unfortunately, Sykes's classes were not always on a schedule, and became even more irregular.

On a warm summer day in 1971, I went to a car wash and needed change. I asked a guy if he had some quarters for a dollar bill. His name was Richard "Dick" Lopez, and he recognized my family name and knew my relatives. Turns out he was one of the earliest from the Erie area to study with Willem Reeders. When we met, Lopez was teaching kuntao-silat in a small studio behind the home of another Reeders student, ex-marine Raymond Cunningham (1928–2008). He invited me to visit his school.

As it turned out, Lopez was a gem of a martial artist and, more important, proved to be a man of rare character. I can call him a true friend for life. He began his studies with karate and judo in Erie, Pennsylvania. His judo skills benefited by studies in Germany while he was serving in the military. When he returned to the United States, he heard that Willem Reeders was teaching judo and karate in Jamestown, New York. Lopez went to meet him, was impressed with his judo, and traveled weekly to study with him. They developed a good friendship through their joy of judo practice and humor. When Reeders decided to stop teaching judo and start teaching kuntao, Lopez decided to study the new curriculum. Others followed Lopez to study with Reeders.

Lopez would take my kuntao-silat studies to a higher level, but more important, he was a living example of what martial arts entailed, technically and theoretically. Although I chose not to wear any belts, he presented me with an orange sash (black belt level). The sash is valuable to me, not as any symbol of rank, but for what it specifically means coming from this person I respect. It represents a part of Lopez's own tradition.

Lopez was well trained. He would teach—showing what he learned and explaining where the techniques came from—but he always would point out the limits of what he was absolutely sure about regarding style, technique, and history.

Sykes and Lopez both studied closely with Reeders. When in Erie, Reeders often stayed at the Lopez home. As first-generation students, Sykes and Lopez eventually started teaching, and the methodology used was similar to their teacher's. Most of Reeders' classes focused on learning the movements in a technique and its application, and perhaps some variations. Students individually practiced the movements repetitively for much of the class time. The same techniques were later practiced with a partner, repeated for months until the techniques became fluid. Speed intensified and control became more and more precise. Forms were taught, but there was a lot of sparring. Reeders was quite fluent with a variety of weapons, a favorite being the *taichu* (Japanese, *sai*) (Dohrenwend, 2002). However, it seems he shared only part of his repertoire with selected students.

Lopez eventually lessened the intensity of the teaching regimen. Sykes also changed over the years by embellishing whenever he liked. For example, he created a number of routines from the individual techniques he learned from Reeders. In "karate tournaments" during the 1960s, Sykes would state the kata's name—which he had just made up—and then spontaneously perform for judges. If asked to repeat the routine, of course he'd opt to perform a different one! Very creative.

The common thread in Reeders's teachings—clearly exemplified through the way Sykes, Lopez, Cunningham, and Pepperman viewed the art—is practicality. Theory and practice had one objective, which was to devastate an opponent or opponents as quickly and severely as possible. Lopez said Reeders often referred to his methods as "dirty fighting." There was nothing nice or compassionate about them. There was little pushing or restraining, but there were plenty of finger strikes to the eyes, throat, and groin areas. Blocks were usually not simply blocks, but were employed to break bone or cripple. Neck, vertebrae, and joints were targeted for quick breaks. Defense and attack blended into one concept where the mind and body moved spontaneously as needed.

The goal for a kuntao-silat practitioner is to end any confrontation quickly. Combative encounters are not prolonged exhibitions of skills, as so commonly shown in the movie industry. Two fundamental guidelines for Indonesian systems are to evade any attack and to incapacitate the attacker. In most cases, one can evade an attack by moving the body away or turning at angles to deflect or neutralize the opponent's movement. Incapacitating an attacker is usually accomplished by attacking soft vital areas, such as the eyes, ears, throat, groin, and joints. Highly skilled masters evade and attack simultaneously at lightning speed.

Thoughts on Kuntao-Silat

At the start of this article, we asked what traits distinguish kuntao-silat from other Asian martial arts. The natural starting point for this inquiry is Indonesia's geographic setting as the crucible where kuntao-silat developed and where it was nurtured through contributions from three main cultures: (1) native, (2) Indian, and (3) Chinese. Considering that this archipelago includes hundreds of islands and many ethnic groups, there has been a history of strife at the village and regional levels for nearly two millennia. Over the centuries, the sociopolitical pressures among groups made martial art study a priority.

The ancient native culture included animistic beliefs and a physical regimen that suited the Southeast Asian body type and lifestyle in the equatorial tropics. Sufi mysticism from India, as well as Chinese Daoist beliefs, blended to give kuntao-silat unique psychological tools that infused their fighting arts. An example is how the mesmerizing music of a gamelan ensemble can enhance the hypnotic, deathly dance of a Pukulan silat practitioner. Actually, kuntao-silat is often practiced with musical accompaniment.

The practice of Chinese animal styles was animated by the very presence of dangerous and cunning animals living in the Indonesian jungles, such as the fierce sun bear, Komodo dragon, Sumatran tiger, and numerous species of snakes and monkeys. Chinese kuntao mixed with silat, and both no doubt were also tinged with theories and practices from India, such as the fighting art of kalarippayattu.

All people living on the Indonesian islands have blended a variety of cultural streams to form their own unique identities. Martial artists in Indonesia manifested their arts with differences, much the way that faces of members in one family reflect their own identities. Indonesian martial arts are largely individualistic hybrid styles containing elements of body movement found also in Indonesian-style dance and theater. When we look at any form of kuntao-silat, we see movement inspired by a deep seated mind-set which is also unique to the archipelago. This deals with the survival instinct and a physical and psychological need to possess a highly practical fighting art. For example, those of an indigenous group called the Dayak in Kalimantan province on Borneo were famed head-hunters. Their trophies remind us that the origin and purpose of martial arts were focused on life and death realities of combat. Such arts are not practiced for sport and will never gain great popularity.

As author, I can only write from my own experience with kuntao-silat. Here we looked briefly at the teachings of Willem Reeders as viewed through my studies with Arthur Sykes and Richard Lopez, contacts with others familiar with Reeders, and with some supporting published books and articles dealing with kuntao-silat. It is apparent that Reeders and many Indonesian martial art masters studied with a variety of teachers and mixed styles into their own hybrid systems. The de Thouars brothers certainly did this too.

Most martial art systems are not as neatly organized with detailed lineage scrolls as those found in Japan. On the contrary, it seems most combative arts have developed ad hoc, infused by experts through fateful circumstances. Generally, Indonesian kuntao-silat systems do not have reliable documentation for their history and evolution. It would be interesting and insightful to have access to details regarding family histories, lineages, reports on how kuntao-silat was utilized over the centuries, and precise overviews of all physical and mental practices associated with particular systems. However, many details are not necessary. What does the art itself exhibit? Effectiveness is the only yardstick for measuring a truly combative system.

Grandmaster Reeders.
Photo by Raymond Cunningham.

In the case of kuntao-silat, we can see and feel the highly effective fighting techniques in the many styles found in Indonesia. We can learn more about the individual styles: Cimande, Pencak Silat, Bakti Negara, Cikalong, Harimau, Serak, etc. Learning even a little about such arts will certainly prove insightful for those practicing and researching other Asian styles that have either lost their original combative foundations or have focused on other aspects, such as health, sport, or entertainment.

In addition to its near-mystic mental states, distinguishing traits of kuntao-silat can be seen in its beautiful, dancelike fluidity of movement; human imitation of animal stances accompanied by panther clawing, gorilla striking, evasive monkey stepping, and snake-darting finger strikes. All such traits organically combine in kuntao-silat styles to embody radar sensitivity to spontaneously face any realistic combative situation.

Bibliography

Alexander, H., Chambers, Q., and Draeger, D. (1974). *Pentjak-silat: The Indonesian fighting art.* Tokyo: Kodansha International Ltd.

Chambers, Q. and Draeger, D. (1979). *Javanese silat: The fighting art of Perisai Diri.* Tokyo: Kodansha International Ltd.

Cordes, H. (1990). Pencak silat: Die kampfkunst der Minangkabau und ihr kulturelles umfeld. Ph.D. dissertation, University of Cologne, Germany.

Davies, P. (2000). Kuntao: Cultural marginality in Indo-Malay martial tradition. *Journal of Asian Martial Arts,* 9(2): 28–47.

Dohrenwend, R. (2002). The odd East Asian sai. *Journal of Asian Martial Arts,* 11(3): 8–29.

Draeger, D. (1972). *The weapons and fighting arts of Indonesia.* Rutland, VT: Tuttle Publishing.

Draeger, D. and Smith, R. (1969). *Comprehensive Asian fighting arts.* New York: Kodansha America.

Farrer, D. (2009). *Shadows of the prophet: Martial arts and Sufi mysticism.* Berlin, Germany: Springer.

Maliszewski, M. (1992). Meditative-religious traditions of fighting arts and martial ways. *Journal of Asian Martial Arts,* 1(3): 1–104. See subheading on "Indonesia," pages 26–29.

Maliszewski, M. (1990). Personal videotape recordings taken through Asia, including Indonesia.

Parker, C. (1995). Introduction to the welcoming postures of pencak silat. *Journal of Asian Martial Arts,* 4(4): 84–101.

Pauka, K. (2003). Silat-based Randai theater of West Sumatra makes its U.S. debut. *Journal of Asian Martial Arts,* 12(1): 48–65.

Pauka, K. (1999). Randai and silek: Folk theatre and martial arts of the Minangkabau in West Sumatra. CD-ROM. University of Michigan Press.

Pauka, K. (1998). *Theater and martial arts in West Sumatra: Randai and silek of the Minangkabau.* Ohio University Press.

Pauka, K. (1997). Silek: The martial arts of the Minangkabau in West Sumatra. *Journal of Asian Martial Arts,* 6(1): 62–79.

Pauka, K. (1996). A flower of martial arts: The Randai folk theatre of the Minangkabau in West Sumatra. *Journal of Asian Martial Arts,* 6(4): 10–29.

Pauka, K. (1995). Martial arts, magic, and male bonding: The pauleh tinggi ceremony in West Sumatra. *Journal of Asian Martial Arts,* 4(3): 26–45.

Wilson, J. (1993). Chasing the magic: Mysticism and the martial arts on the island of Java. *Journal of Asian Martial Arts,* 2(2): 10–43.

Chapter II

Yang and Chen Taijiquan: Universal Principles

Yang Qingyu's Compassionate Presence

While attending Edinboro State University, I took a semester of Mandarin along with sixteen other students. The following semester's Mandarin II consisted of myself and one other student. I learned that the instructor, Harold Zhou, had studied Dong Style Taijiquan when he lived in China. Originally from the northern city of Tianjin, Professor Zhou moved to Hong Kong where he studied with the famous Dong Yingjie (1898-1961). He appreciated my love of Chinese culture and in 1973 began to teach me taiji in an empty college classroom. He patiently taught me the traditional long routine. After I graduated in 1975, I would pay weekly visits to his home in Edinboro. He had retired and hopefully enjoyed our talks as much as I did. His wife Daisy would usually serve tea or sometimes make lunch. His flawless technique in picking up a single peanut with chopsticks is an admired skill.

Professor Zhou is responsible for another life-changing event: introducing me to a taijiquan teacher in Taiwan. Zhou had a close friend in Taipei studying with Master Yang Qingyu (楊清玉 1915-2002). They made a formal introduction for me to begin studies with him. I decided to first go to India to visit former classmates and see some cultural spots and the majestic Himalayas. I departed on June 19, 1976 and arrived in Taipei a month later.

Yang was born in Song Village (宋莊), which is located in Sheqi county (社旗县) in the southwestern side of Henan Province. Song Village is about 150 miles from the Shaolin Temple, and 200 miles to Chen Village (birthplace of taiji). Yang was a military officer who came to Taiwan following the civil war in

Yang Qingyu.

which Mao Zedong and the Communist Party founded the People's Republic of China on the mainland and Chiang Kai-shek established the Republic of China on Taiwan. In Taiwan, Yang had been a senior student under another ex-military officer, Grandmaster Xiong Yanghe (1886-1984), one of the most respected martial art masters in Taiwan, teaching Shaolin boxing and Yang Taiji.

For Yang's taiji class, we'd meet Monday thru Friday every morning at Taipei's New Park (now called 228 Peace Memorial Park) just before sunrise. Master Yang would arrive with a dozen students waiting in anticipation. Worn over the years of practice, the ground was soft dirt. Although Yang wore no uniform or insignia or rank, people always showed utmost respect for him as a person and as a teacher.

After some chatting and stretching, we'd start the traditional Yang Style long routine. After twenty-five minutes it took to complete, students would practice by themselves or sometimes in pairs. They patiently worked to improve their movements in the solo routine and straight sword form, or the two-person routines and exercises of push-hands (*tuishou*) and a two-person duet called "dispersing hands" (*sanshou*).

As he did with other students, Yang taught me one movement at a time. The instruction was primarily visual. I'd watch, mimic his movements, and watch closer. I didn't know if I'd get to return to Taiwan, so I made every second count.

Whenever he felt the urge, Yang would step in to offer suggestions, show a new movement, illustrate the correct way of performing a movement, or demonstrate a function. We never sparred, but Master Yang must have had much hands-on training when he was younger. With one hand, he could quickly and accurately place an excruciating thumb-lock on you that would affect your whole body. After witnessing such techniques, it was apparent that Yang developed skills through training methods not seen in his public classes held at the park. One time, while learning a new movement, I was holding one of my hands too low to protect myself, so he smacked me lightly in the head. I never again forgot where my hand should be in that particular posture and paid closer attention to even the seemingly minor aspects of every movement in the routine.

The students were of varied ages and backgrounds, but most were older. Some were retirees, such as a woman who was a retired high school principal, and a frail but always smiling gentleman who was learning to gain strength. A few were younger people in the work force or college who would come for the refreshing morning exercise before going off to jobs or to school. I was the youngest and the only foreigner. We got to know each other well because it was usual for us to talk for a while after class.

Classes never really ended. Students dispersed according to their own timing, going off to work, school, or home. But there was always a group of us that would go off together for breakfast. A leisurely breakfast provided time not only to discuss taiji, but to learn of each individual's personality and background. We often met at other times for lunches, dinners, visiting family homes, or sightseeing.

Yang had a simple teaching methodology, very informal, but well organized. Confucian ideals concerning proper manners—such as appropriateness of behavior between teacher, student, and classmates—were the common essentials that created a bond withing the group. Mr. Yang taught, but it was up to the student to grasp his instructions. Each progressed according to his or her own capacity and innate talents. Mr. Yang was always there to nurture.

Where the author studied with Master Yang in 1976,
228 Peace Memorial Park, Taipei, Taiwan.

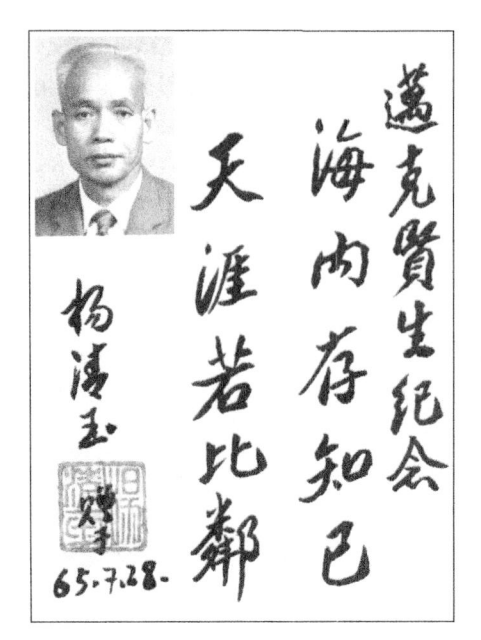

Above left, gift from Master Yang: "Regardless of the ocean depths or the vastness of the sky, friendship is close." Right, in front of a statue of Gen. Chennault in 228 Peace Memorial Park, 1976. Chennault was an American military aviator who commanded the "Flying Tigers" during World War II in China.

Left, Master Yang at the Guanyin (Goddess of Mercy) Buddhist Temple, May 21, 1989.
Below at a park in Puli.

Article adapted from the *Journal of Asian Martial Arts*, Vol. 18 No. 3
Xiong Yanghe's Taiji in Taiwan

In the thickly branched tree representing taijiquan's growth over the centuries, some branches are stronger than others, and some hold higher positions than others. Here we introduce a relatively rare branch in the Yang Family tradition that is associated with Xiong Yanghe (熊養和 1888-1981). We will look closely at the two main branches that stem directly from the Yang Style founder, Yang Luchan (1799-1872), his sons and grandsons, who were so influential in the initial growth of taiji in China.

Early Yang Style Lineage Representatives

Yang Luchan was born in 1799 in Yongnian County, Hebei Province. He moved to Beijing where he gained a reputation as "Invincible Yang" and taught the Manchu royal family and bodyguards. Of course, his unique flavor of taiji became known as the Yang Style.

When Yang Luchan died in 1872, two of his sons carried on the family's taiji tradition. Yang Banhou (1837-1890), the elder son, had a character often described as hard and fierce, which manifested in his love of sparring. The younger son, Yang Jianhou (1839-1917), was friendly and gentle, a personality which attracted a large number of students.

Although Yang Shaohou (1862-1930) was the first son of Yang Jianhou, Shaohou studied primarily with his uncle, Yang Banhou. Shaohou followed his uncle in temperament and fighting style. Both were harsh teachers and only a relatively small number of students became dedicated disciples.

Yang Jianhou's second son was Yang Chengfu (1883-1936). He and his brother Shaohou taught taijiquan at the Beijing Physical Culture Research Institute from 1914 until 1928. They were pioneers in bringing instruction to the general public. Chengfu's particular style became the most widespread. Chengfu's public style became popular for its health nurturing benefits.

Xiong Yanghe and His Unique Contributions to Taijiquan

What is Xiong Yanghe's place in this development? Within the Yang Taijiquan linage, he took his teachings to Taiwan following the exodus of the Chinese Nationalists to Taiwan in 1949 and became a major influence in the spread of taiji throughout the island. When he passed away in 1981, he and his senior disciples had taught over ten thousand students. His style continues to spread via his disciples, and his unique system is now referred to as Xiong Style Taiji. Xiong's story proves interesting for his unique place in taiji as well as his personal life.

Xiong was born on September 29, 1888 in Jiangsu Province, in Funing County. His father, Xiong Weizhen, passed the provincial examination (*juren* military degree) during the late Qing Dynasty. Yanghe studied martial arts first with his father, then his father hired instructors for his young son: at age 12, a Shaolin master named Liu He and his disciple Liu Zhongfang came to teach; at age 15, Master Yin Wanbang for Jiangnan Eight Harmonies Boxing system. These had a martial influence from Gan Fengchi. When Xiong was 20, "Miraculous Hand" Tang Dianqing (1850-1926) was hired to teach. These teachers provided young Xiong with an excellent foundation in Shaolin boxing and may have given Xiong his first exposure to taijiquan.

Xiong had hands-on fighting experience as he helped his father maintain township security. He found himself all too often fighting with gangsters. When he was 19 years old, he was the local boxing champion in the "no holds barred" competitions held on raised platforms (*leitai*), as seen in the movie *Fearless*. Because of his powerful kicks, Xiong earned the nickname of "Funing Legs." Such experiences gave him boxing insights, but he was destined to enrich his martial arts by contacts made through his work.

When Xiong was 23 years old, he began a career in the military, which dealt with security and military operations. At 29, he was Adjunct Director of the Anhui Province government office, and at 35 he went on to a management position in the Funing County garrisons. During this period, Xiong met Old Frame Yang Style Taijiquan master Hu Puan (1878-1947), who became his most influential teacher. Hu's nickname was "Hu Hu," meaning "Tiger Hu."

Hu was born in Anhui Province, Jing County. He served as the Department Chief of Jiangsu Province Civil Administration. As a sinologist well-known for his books and poetry, Hu taught at Shanghai University. While in Shanghai, he had an opportunity to meet and study with a number of high caliber taiji masters. He practiced daily starting at 6:00am for over 18 years, until he became disabled by a stroke and resulting paralysis.[1]

Who was Hu's primary taiji teacher? Sources differ, stating he studied with:

1) Chen Weiming (1881-1958)[2]
2) Yang Jianhou (1839-1917)[3]
3) Yang Chengfu (1883-1936)[4]
4) Yang Shaohou (1862-1930)[5]
5) Le Huanzhi (1899-1960)[6]

Most statements regarding Hu Puan's teachers simply say that he studied with this particular person or that one. Furthermore, there are questions about the length of time that Hu studied with his teachers. What could he have learned from them? One reference says "Yang Chengfu and disciple Mr. Hu Puan . . . compared notes together, making a thorough study of taijiquan, gaining thorough and penetrating insights into taiji gongfu."[7] To state that Hu was Yang Chengfu's "disciple" is a strong statement. Unfortunately, I have not found solid evidence to substantiate this pronouncement.

Hu Puan probably met all of these teachers and may have studied with each to different degrees. But it is interesting to note that he spoke so highly of Le Huanzhi (1899-1960), who was from Gushi County in Henan. Le was a medical doctor and also a senior disciple of Dong Yingjie (1898-1961). In his published memoir, Hu wrote that Le's taijiquan is extremely fine. Hu wrote that—from his own push-hands experience with Yang Chengfu, Sun Lutang, Wu Jianquan, and Le Huanzhi—Le proved superior, and his touch was highly effective yet had an undetectable source, "like passing clouds and flowing water," "as not having matter."[8]

Because the sources are obscure, it is difficult to know from whom Hu Puan received his taijiquan instruction. Also, the lineage for Xiong has not been evenly defined. There are a few sources that state that Xiong was a disciple of Yang Shaohou.[9] This seems to be an assumption based primarily on what Xiong taught. However, both Xiong and Hu Puan probably had some contact with Yang Shaohou. What we do know for sure is that, in his autobiography (1962), Xiong himself only mentions Hu Puan in regards to the transmission of the Yang Style Old Frame. This does not negate the possibility that Xiong met other Yang Style Taiji masters, or learned their methods via Hu Puan.

Xiong may have "studied thoroughly with Hu Puan," but he no doubt did have good relations with other taijiquan masters.[10] One source states that Xiong had the chance to meet Yang Jianhou while staying in Beijing for official business. It gave him the opportunity to seek advice about taijiquan, especially regarding the two-person routine call *sanshou* ("dispersing hands"). At this time, Xiong studied wholeheartedly and was able to grasp the deeper mysteries of the art.[11] Yet another source mentions that Yang Jianhou taught in Funing County, and Xiong sought his advice for the sanshou practice.[12] Liang Dongcai (aka, T.T. Liang) states that Yang Jianhou taught Xiong sanshou. Liang also maintains that nobody could have possibly learned it from Yang Chengfu, because his father Yang Jianhou died before he could teach it to him (Hayward, 2000: 61).

Since Xiong had to take part in policy discussions falling within the range of his official military duties, he had a great opportunity to meet many people who were highly skilled in a variety of martial traditions. They could compare their studies and benefit by observing the full scope of Chinese martial arts. Over the decades, Xiong received a solid grounding in Northern and Southern Shaolin and taijiquan from his personal teachers and from contact with others through his military career. Here are some highlights from his career:[13]

Age   *Position*
39   Regimental Commander, Revolutionary Army
40   Jiangsu Province Funing County Public Security Bureau Chief, and concurrent position as Production Brigade Chief
49   Jiangsu Province Funing County Magistrate
52   Security Major General Brigade Commander
53   Security Assistant Commandant
54   Security Major General Commander
58   Major General Group Commander
60   Deputy Commanding Officer, Military Headquarters

In 1949, the Communist Party established the People's Republic of China (PRC) on the mainland. Xiong resigned and moved to Taiwan when "nearly 600,000 Nationalist troops and their dependents withdrew from the mainland to Taiwan."[14] It is commonly said that part of this migratory wave included four famed "Big Dogs" of taijiquan: Zheng Manqing (1901-1975), Guo Lianying, Shi Diaomei and Xiong Yanghe.

After settling in Yilan city in 1953, Xiong tirelessly taught taiji. Eventually, Xiong Style practitioners came to number over 10,000. Xiong's most significant contribution to taiji's legacy is the thorough preservation and transmission of Yang Taijiquan as a fighting art and exercise system, most notably being the two-person practice of sanshou.

In addition, his books leave a detailed record of the system.

Even in his twilight years, Xiong was up daily at 4:30 am to start his day, which included his regular taiji classes. In addition to chanting Buddhist scriptures, practicing brush calligraphy, and reading military history, he wrote books, which leave a detailed record of the taiji system for following generations. He was a Buddhist who treated his disciples with a fatherly affection. He died on October 29, 1981 in Yilan Yuan Shan Rongmin Hospital at the age of 94.

Formal photo of Grandmaster Xiong with students.
February 1, 1970.

Xiong Yanghe's Curriculum

On the Neijia Formosa website, David Chesser writes this regarding Xiong's curriculum: "This amount of training makes it the most complete version of taiji practiced on the island. I simply haven't found anything that compares to it."[15]

- Yang Family Old Frame Xiong Style Taijiquan (111 style)
- Taiji Basic (standing) Post
- Taiji Qigong
- Push-hands (*tuishou*)
- Dispersing Hands (*sanshou*)
- Taiji sword
- knife
- stick
- staff
- paired swords (two-person)
- paired knives (two-person)
- paired sticks (two-person)
- paired staves (two-person)
- Six Directions Flower Spear (*Liulu Huaqiang*)
- Spring and Autumn broadsword
- double swords
- Mizong Boxing
- Four Gates Hong Boxing
- Young Hong Boxing
- Sunlight Palm (*Ziyang Zhang Deng*)

Concluding Remarks on Xiong Style Taijiquan

Most taiji styles today have evolved away from their martial roots. Xiong Style offers combative elements that were necessary during the extreme chaos found in China during the early Yang Family transmissions of the art.

This brief overview of Xiong Style helps define and give meaning to the words "taijiquan." Taiji is not just an exercise and not only a fighting art. It is both, and its dual nature is inherent in the teachings of true masters. One who has mastered Xiong's system, or the early Yang Family systems, can impart the theory and knowledge applicable in both areas as a combative art and exercise system. The mix is largely determined by the teacher-student relationship and the motives involved. Yang Family Xiong Style Taijiquan gives us an unique opportunity to look back in time when the template of Yang Style was forged. As the system thrives in Taiwan under Xiong's disciples and their own disciples—teachers such as Lin Jianhong and Lin Chaolai—we see that the old system has been preserved, while even spreading outside Taiwan to benefit others. It's a taste of "old wine in a new bottle."

References – Website Sources

[1] http://yuehuanzhi.blog.sohu.com
[2] www.taiji.net.cn/liu/wlys/200712/6426.shtml; http://yuehuanzhi.blog.sohu.com
[3] http://blog.udn.com/article/trackback.jsp?uid=wang6196192001&aid=1077817
[4] http://tw.myblog.yahoo.com/q3taichi/article?mid=23&sc=1
[5] http://library.taiwanschoolnet.org; http://blog.youthwant.com.tw/vadjra/vadjra/6395839/
[6] http://yuehuanzhi.blog.sohu.com; www.xici.net/u6819319/d19792891.htm
[7] http://tw.myblog.yahoo.com/q3taichi/profile
[8] www.xici.net/u6819319/d19792891.htm
[9] www.dotaichi.com
[10] http://blog.sina.com.tw/lkk_blog/article.php?pbgid=36074&entryid=320007
[11] http://www.lin-gi.com.tw/discuss/Viewtopic.asp?SubjectID=7135&Sign=150
[12] http://tw.myblog.yahoo.com/jin_cang/article?mid=1003&prev=2170&next=554&=f&fid=3
[13] http://blog.udn.com/wang6196192001/1067085
[14] http://taiwanreview.nat.gov.tw/fp.asp?xItem=589&CtNode=128
[15] http://chessman71.wordpress.com/2006/05/15/yang-shao-houstaiji/)

References – Chinese

ANONYMOUS, (1987). *Mr. Xiong's 100th birthday commemorative special edition*. (n.p.).

ANONYMOUS , (1984). *National arts master Xiong Yanghe commemorative collection*. (n.p.).

LIN, CAOLAI (2007). *Yang family old frame Xiong style taijiquan*. DVD. Yilan, Taiwan: Chin-yu Martial Art Study Association.

YANG, QINGYU (1976). *Xiong style taijiquan long form, push-hands, and sword form*. Private film collection.

YANG, QINGYU (1988). *Autobiography*. Self published.
YANG, QINGYU (n.d.). *A brief biography of Xiong Yanghe*. Self published.
XIONG, Y.H. (1962). *Autobiography*. Self published.
XIONG, Y.H. (1963). *The taijiquan explained*. Taipei: Taiwan China Book Printing House.
XIONG, Y.H. (1971). *Taiji swordsmanship illustrated*. Yilan, Taiwan: Lu Feng Printing and Publishing House.
XIONG, Y.H. (1975). *The taijiquan explained*. 3rd edition. Taipei: Huge Distribution Planning Company.

References - English

DEMARCO, M. (1992). The origin and evolution of taijiquan. *Journal of Asian Martial Arts, 1*(1): 8-25.
HUCKER, C. (1975). *China's imperial past: An introduction to Chinese history and culture*. Stanford, CA: Stanford University Press.
GALLAGHER, P. (2007). *Drawing silk: Masters' secrets for successful tai chi practice*. Charleston, SC: BookSurge.
HAYWARD, R. (2000). *T'ai-chi ch'uan: Lessons with master T.T. Liang*. St. Paul, MN: Shu-Kuang Press.
KUHN, P. (1970). *Rebellion and its enemies in late imperial China: Militarization and social structure, 1796-1864*. Cambridge, MA: Harvard University Press.
KURLAND, H. (May 1998). "Hsiung Yang-Ho's san shou form." *T'ai chi Ch'uan and Wellness Newsletter*. Downloaded July 16, 2009.
KURLAND, H. (2003). "History of a rare t'ai-chi form: San shou." http://www.self-growth.com/articles/Kurland3.html. Downloaded July 16, 2009.
LU, S. (Yun, Z., Trans.) (2006). *Combat techniques of taiji, xingyi, and bagua*. Berkeley, CA: Blue Snake Books.
OLSON, S. (1999). *T'ai chi thirteen sword: A sword master's manual*. Burbank, CA: Multi-Media Books.
OLSON, S. (1999). *T'ai chi sensing-hands: A complete guide to t'ai chi t'ui-shou training from original Yang Family records*. Burbank, CA: Multi-Media Books.
OLSON, S. (1992). *The teachings of master T.T. Liang: Imagination becomes reality, the complete guide to the 150 posture solo form*. St. Paul, MN: Dragon Door Publications.
RUSSELL, J. (2004). *The tai chi two-person dance: Tai chi with a partner*. Berkeley, CA: North Atlantic Books.
SHERIDAN, J. (1977). *China in disintegration: The Republican Era in Chinese

> *history 1912-1949*. New York: The Free Press.
> SCHURMANN, F. AND SCHELL, O. (1967). *Republican China: Nationalism, war, and the rise of communism 1911-1949*. New York: Vintage Book.
> WAKEMAN, F. (1977). *The fall of imperial China*. New York: The Free Press.
> WILE, D. (1996). *T'ai-chi touchstones: Yang family secret transmissions*. Brooklyn, NY: Sweet Chi Press.

A Unicorn Appears: Chen Taiji Stylist Du Yuze

It had been a few years since I graduated from Edinboro University with a bachelor's degree. With my Asian travels, Mandarin and martial art studies, it dawned on me that I should return to academia for a Master of Arts Degree in Asian Studies. Seton Hall University was excellent, providing a solid foundation, particularly for China, Japan, and Korea. My focus was on China and Daoism. Graduating in 1981, I wondered just how the coursework would influence my future.

The following few years I worked some odd jobs and started writing articles on Asian-related topics. On the martial traditions, my first published piece appeared in *Black Belt* magazine, then other periodicals including, *Inside Karate*, *Inside Kung Fu*, and *Internal Arts*. It felt good to be productive, using skills and information from both martial art and academic studies. But work took time aways from studies!

Returning to Taiwan in 1984, I had two objectives: to study at the Taiwan National Normal University's Mandarin Training Center, and dive deeper into the martial arts. I quickly learned that the mode of taiji instruction had changed. Master Yang had departed the thoroughly modernized capital of Taipei and moved to a mountain monastery in Puli—at the geographic center of Taiwan, where the air and water were the purest on the island. He retreated from the growing disrespect found among the newer, youthful students and those taiji associates where were clamoring for fame and money through commercial means.

Since I was staying in Taipei, I couldn't meet with Yang. One of my classmates under Yang, Tu Zongren, introduced me to Du Yuze (杜毓澤 1896-1990), one of the rare Chen style taiji masters in Taiwan. Du's father was governor of the area near Chen Village, the birthplace of taiji. The top master of the time was Chen Yenxi who left the village to take employment as the Du Family's personal bodyguard. Du Yuze became his student —a significant event since at that time Chen Taiji was still surrounded by secrecy and taught mainly to family members.

Governor Du Yomei sitting with family, including son Du Yuze, back row, center.

I worked on Chen Style's First Routine for the year. I spent much time with Tu Zongren, who was one of four senior students who were "adopted" by Du. Tu would treat patients with acupuncture and I got to observe the sessions. In between sessions, we'd practice. Or, we just met to practice. Other times we'd go to Du's home and practice in his livingroom. Usually it would just be Tu and I there, but on occasion there'd be a few other students. When I returned to the United States, I had enough to work on.

At home in Pennsylvania, I returned to writing projects and some part-time work. It wasn't easy to find work that could utilize my background in Asian Studies. In 1988, I found work as a Tour Director for Inter-Pacific Tours, the largest tour company dealing with China at the time. I escorted tour groups to various Asian locations, mainly China. This placed me in a leadership role working with local guides for each city, and handling medical and other problems that regularly occurred. Familiarity with the culture facilitates such work. This was a nice opportunity to travel much of Asia, seeing and learning about the cultures first-hand. We stayed in great hotels. Went to wonderful restaurants.

The company specialized on China tours. Itineraries included the main tourist cities: Shanghai, Hangzhou, Beijing, Xi'an, Guilin, and usually ended in Hong Kong. Fortune brought me to other areas around China too, such as Harbin, Kunming, Chongqing, Chungdu, Suzhou, Guangzhou, and Nanjing. We went on crusies on the Yangzi River and the Li River that flows through the magical mountains surrounding Guilin city. This work brought book learning to life. The cultural sites spanned all of Chinese civilization from 6,000 year old neolithic sites to the modern Beijing subway system. Each city was different in dialects, foods, clothing styles and even different martial arts.

Following the couple years serving as a Tour Director, I returned to Taiwan from mid-1989 to mid-1990. On the academic side, I received a grant from the Pacific Cultural Foundation to conduct research on various aspects of Daoism. Of course I returned to review Chen Style's first routine and could now start to learn the second routine called Cannon Fist.

Usually only two or three students would practice in front of Master Du, who sat in his livingroom chair, watching, and making corrections. In 1989 he was already 92 or 93 years old. He loved his art and, perhaps because he had an engineering background, he had a good way of describing the kinetics of techniques and the fluctuations between yin and yang. If he couldn't explain in words, he'd get out of the chair to demonstrate, sometimes in very low stances.

In a hallway just off the livingroom, there was a hardwood board that looked like a solid picture frame on the wall. Du said: "Come. Watch. Listen." We went close to the board and I noticed that the bottom of the board was slightly away from the wall. Behind the board was a section of a thick metal car spring. This was a punching board! I inspected it and tried to push the board to close the gap, but the board wouldn't budge.

Standing in front of the board, Du threw a "hidden fist" strike, hitting the board with the first two largest knuckles. The force from his punch caused the board to "clap" as it hit the wall. I was in shock to see such an elderly man do this. Then he did it with an elbow strike. The third technique was a shoulder strike, but I didn't hear a click that time. This day I remember well because it was so inspiring—not the techniques, but the master's spirit.

Tu Zongren studied with Yang Qingyu and Du Yuze, so we were often together. One evening we were on way to his home. As we were driving along the boulevard on a busy Taipei street, he made a left-hand turn. Trees and bushes limited the view of a speeding car that hit us broadside. Two couples were in a hurry to get to a movie theater. The dapper driver got out of the car, saying he needed to call his brother who owned it. Fifteen minutes later a car showed up with five men inside. His brother was not inside. These were clearly five thugs.

Zongren and the biggest thug started to argue. Words turned into finger pointing, leading to shoving each other. Every time the thug attacked, Zongren would deflect him away. After this happened a number of times, another thug joined in. Zongren kept deflecting and throwing. Then a third joined in. Three against one. The leader asked his accomplices if he should take out a knife. Anyone caught in Taiwan using a knife gets a long jail term, so no knife came out. A fourth man joined. Zongren was doing fine, but I started to move toward the melee to help. The driver, keeping calm and puffing on a cigarette, told me not to enter. If I did, it would become an international incident. I saw Zongren hit the leader in the mouth with a leopard strike, cutting the inside of his mouth on his own teeth.

Zongren, who was wearing dress shoes, slipped and fell. I ran over and stood next to him with my right arm stretched out over his body to keep the leader away. Most of my weight was in my left leg with my right leg facing the leader. Just then, a smaller man darted toward me, throwing a right punch toward my left temple. I didn't block. As his punch came closer, I started to shift away. I could feel his knuckles touch my temple. Moving at the same speed as his strike, the punch made absolutely no impact. I only shifted to my right leg and looked him in the eyes. I didn't want to do as Zongren, only deflecting and throwing, and perhaps run out of luck trying to defend. My idea was that the attacker had one chance, and it failed. There should not be a second chance. If attacked again, I'd do my best to end the fight immediately. The thug backed off. Nobody would attack again.

The situation was serious. Zongren could have been injured by being too reserved. The leader disappeared. The rest of us needed to go to the police station for questioning. The driver had to pay for repairs to Zongren's car. This incident was one of the biggest tests of my martial arts. Could I remain calm during conflict? Move appropriately in a scuffle? Do what is ethical?

I also managed to make a trip to Puli city to visit Master Yang. There was big talk that he had found a special lady friend a few years prior. He was in his early 70s. Since about two million men went to Taiwan after the Civil War (1945-1949), most men didn't have the opportunity to marry. Yang had a bed at her home but often would stay at a Buddhist temple, where he would teach monks. During my visit, he went in the evenings to sleep at the temple, and let me use his own bed at the house. Looking back over the decades, I feel the friendships with my teachers have been among life's greatest blessings.

The last time I visited Taiwan was in 2017 to attend a celebration of

Master Du Yuze practicing sword in Boai, China.

the 130th anniversary of Grandmaster Xiong Yanghe. I was asked to write an article for it to be published in a commemorative book. I hadn't sent foot in Taiwan for twenty-eight years. Incredible changes. I was happy to see that living conditions improved immensely. Most noticable was how the populous progressed over the years into a truely civil society. Today Taiwan is recognized as one of friendliest countries for travelers to visit. Although I didn't personally know the present-day masters of the Xiong system, they treated me like a brother, welcomed me in their homes, shared taiji books and information, went to dinners, etc. In large part, this treatment was in respect for my teacher, whom they all knew.

Article adapted from the *Journal of Asian Martial Arts*, Vol. 1 No. 1
A Brief Description of Chen Style Master Du Yuze
by Wong Jiaxiang (M. DeMarco, Trans.)

Introduction

The following translation is an excerpt from *Master Du Yuze's Eighty-Second Birthday Commemorative Book*, originally written by Wong Jiaxiang. I have chosen to translate part of this booklet for a number of reasons. One reason was to commemorate the 94th birthday Master Du had in 1989.

Regardless of age, Master Du was certainly a unique figure in the world of martial arts. Boxing instructors of various styles acknowledge Du Yuze's unique mastery of the Chen system, believing it to be a national treasure. Instructor Adam Hsu compared many Chen styles while in China in 1986. Hsu wrote in a correspondence that "Du's Chen style is indeed a national treasure. Even in Chen Village, the birthplace of taijiquan, you find almost no one teaching Chen style like this."

Along with Du Yuze's unique place in the lineage of Chen style masters, his personal history is likewise quite interesting. Master Du began his martial art training at an early age partly because of his father's high social standing as a government official. During the later years of the Qing Dynasty (1644-1911), when the political and social conditions were not stable, such a position necessitated the need for bodyguards. The Du family lived under constant guard and visitors to their home were limited to close friends, those who had business with Du's father, or hired instructors.

Because of the above conditions, young Du Yuze was able to study with two great teachers: Masters Chen Yenxi and Chen Mingbiao. Under their guidance he learned both the Old Form (*Lao Jia*) and New Form (*Xin Jia*) sets of the Chen system. Oddly enough, because of the strict household formalities, Master Du never met Chen Fake, the son of Chen Yenxi. Incidently, Chen Fake did not practice the New Form, but concentrated solely on the two routines of Lao Jia (the second known as Cannon First, or *Paochui*).

A word regarding Wong Jiaxiang will help explain his interest and insights in writing the *Commemorative Book*. Mr. Wong, along with Mr. Tu Zongren, Mr. Lee Houchen and Mr. Cao Delin represent the four formal students who have performed the traditional ceremony of kowtowing to Master Du. As a result, they were accepted as "sons" within the Chen Taijiquan Family and are numbered as "sons" in that order. This continues the lineage of Chen Yenxi, since Du Yuze was one of his accepted "sons." Mr. Wong Jiaxiang is now nearly seventy years old and continues to teach in the southern Taiwan city of Tainan.

The following translation of Wong's "Brief Description of Master Du Yuze" I hope will provide interesting details in the tradition of a boxing master. Hopefully it will also indicate the deep feeling and dedication necessary to transform the movements into a perfected art form. Those who have been fortunate enough to fall under the tutelage and inspiration of respected Master Du have also accepted the responsibility to pass on the learning in like manner.

Except where noted, the accompanying photographs were taken at Master Du's home on June 8, 1989, while the "sons" of Mr. Tu Zongren were there to receive some additional instruction. Master Du, carefully watching every movement of the students, spoke in a strong clear voice (in Chinese or German!) to make critical remarks. When words were of no use, he stood to demonstrate. His gongfu was certainly impressive as was his kind personality which radiated the wisdom of his years. This combination of gentleman and master made Du Yuze an indubitably rare form of dragon.

Translation

Master Du Yuze, whose secondary given name is Du Qimin, was from Henan Province, Boai prefecture. He was born in the 23rd year of the Qing Dynasty's Emperor Guangxu; in other words, fifteen years before the 1911 founding of the Chinese Republic, between 5:00 and 7:00 p.m.

Now he is more than eighty-two years old and still practices taijiquan regularly.

Du Yuze.

This practice includes Golden Buddha Pounds Pestle, 1,000 Pounds Fall, Shake Foundation and Kick Twice, Concealed-hand Strike, Strike Towards Groin, Stop Opponent with One Heel (left and right), Swing Foot to Double Target, steps, vertical movements, jumps, leaps . . . He practices every kind of movement, clearly and crisply, placing all in good order. The result is a boxing borne on the wind. At the same time, he has achieved great strength and the briskness of sound health. Because Master Du does not give up this practice, he has remained at his prime. Ah! If one can do all of taiji's profound functions, it is possible to make great progress!

In the eighth year of the Chinese Republican period, when the country was finally stabilized (following great political unrest), Du Yuze attended college to study mechanical engineering. Following his studies, he performed engineering duties in the region of northern China. Afterwards, he came to Taiwan and was employed as an engineering specialist and worked secondarily as a factory manager. Passing through these years in this way was a rewarding experience.

Master Du was originally from Henan, Boai prefecture. Chenjiagou, located in Wen prefecture, is less than seventeen miles away. In the late Qing Dynasty, these same areas formed part of what was then the district of Huai Qing prefecture. This rural area had a close-knit society where everybody knew everyone else who lived there.

When he was eighteen years old, Du Yuze kowtowed to Master Chen Yenxi as part of his formal acceptance as a student. Chen Yenxi was the famed sixteenth generation master of the Chen style and grandson of Chen Changxing. Chen Yenxi taught Du Yuze the *Lao Jia* (Old Form) Chen Family system.

The father of Du Yuze was named Du Yomei. Thirty years before the Qing Emperor Guangxu (reign lasted from 1875 to 1908), Du Yomei had the rare fortune of passing the Jinshi Examination (national civil service examination held at the capital) and was awarded the eleventh degree, the second most outstanding rank that could be received from the Hanlin Academy (government examination office). Du Yomei went abroad to study in Japan during the early Republican years (1912-1949). While in government service, he also traveled to the provinces of Guandong and Guanxi.

Du Yomei asked Chen Yenxi's nephew, Chen Mingbiao, to be his bodyguard, plus his family's personal boxing teacher. He did so because Chen Mingbiao was an expert in archery, the spear and other aspects of the martial arts, including the *Lao Jia* (Old Form) Chen Family Taiji and *Paochui* (Cannon Fist). Consequently, Du Yuze was able to study the *Xin Jia* (Old Form) and Paochui styles under his tutelage.

The movements of the Chen Village style of taijiquan are organized in a series, bound together as by a strong silk thread. To elaborate further, the movements are alternating manifestations of fast and slow; varying degrees of hard and soft as well as varying degrees of empty and substantial.

How to execute these principles in their highest degree is a precious secret not easily shown to others, particularly in an agricultural society whose people must work so much while they study. Therefore, the transmission of this knowledge has not been broad.

In Taiwan, those who have received training in Chen Style Taijiquan are as rare as the mythical phoenix or unicorn. In the past, anyone who could perform the Chen style learned it, like Master Du, during the Qing Dynasty. Because of Master Du's deep commitment to this particular boxing art, he feels a great obligation to preserve what he learned. He repeatedly made appeals to others in Taiwan to follow this path. Master Du, desiring not to neglect this duty to pass on his knowledge, teaches as much as possible by demonstration, so later generations can advance accordingly.

At present, taijiquan is flourishing as a fruit from its roots in Chenjiagou, the village in Wen prefecture of Henan province. And yet, just how to do the Chen Style Taijiquan remains a secret. In addition, the excessive secrecy that surrounds it has placed the art on the verge of extinction. The sixteenth generation Master Chen Pinsan, by giving his total attention for thirteen years, collected, structured, organized and eventually published what he could find regarding taijiquan, including pictures, diagrams and stories.

In the preface at the beginning of this book is a remark that Master Du shares with the respected taijiquan elders: "Indications show that efforts are being made to examine and cultivate the principles of yin and yang in equal fashion." This is being done in order to incorporate the theory of the epigram into the performance of taijiquan and thus bring the art to its full realization. But to research, study and actually acquire this special skill requires guidance.

Together with our upcoming generations, we all have to share the responsibility of seeing that Chen Taijiquan can continue to flourish forever without interruption.

Taiwan, 63rd Year of the Republic of China (1974)
Chrysanthemum Month (9th lunar month)
Respectfully your student,
Wong Jiaxiang

Note: On March 16, 1990, Du Yuze peacefully passed away in Taipei Veteran's Hospital at 10:30a.m.

ISSN 01057-8358

VOLUME 1
NUMBER 1
JANUARY 1992

Journal of Asian Martial Arts

Via Media Publishing Company
Erie, Pennsylvania

Chapter III

Via Media Publishing: Pursuing the Middle Way*

Tilling the Field of Asian Martial Arts Study

Returning to the USA from Taiwan in 1990, I was still unsure of what I really wanted to do as an occupation, full-time work that I would enjoy. I thought to teach at an academic institute and sent our resume's, but none were hiring. I sent resumes to some Asia-related institutes and couldn't even get an interview. I continued practicing martial arts, taught part-time, and started to think about all the aspects facing those interested in learning about martial traditions.

Anyone entering the martial arts for the first time jumps into a flowing stream of cultural influences that contributes to how martial arts are perceived and eventually defined. This vision is highly obscured by bias, fads, salesmanship, Hollywood flair, competitive hype, and a plethora of misinformation. Even if the vision is true according to one perspective, say that of martial sports, it usually neglects the completeness of what martial arts are in their entirety. To a large extent, the view of these combative arts is colored by what is found in print media.

When I started studying a martial art in 1965, judo and karate dominated all media. Karate tournaments grew in popularity. In the U.S., most of the information available came from former military personnel who spent a brief time in Japan, particularly in Okinawa, and had some training. Eventually, and under similar situations, information about martial arts in Korea also started to spread. There was little information about other Asian martial art styles. However, a door was kicked open, and interest in the Asian martial traditions grew.

Black Belt magazine (1961) was the first periodical to focus on combatives. Other popular mass-market magazines followed. The movie and television industries also responded to the idea of supply and demand, producing *Kung Fu* (1972–75), *Enter the Dragon* (1973), *The Karate Kid* (1984), and many more movies. Plus, book titles experienced exponential growth. There were some brilliant flashes of insight and substance in these varied forms of media, enmeshed in various degrees of myth, fantasy, fiction, hyperbole, and misinformation. How could anyone discern fact from fiction regarding the true history and culture of Asian combative traditions?

Publications serve as primary reference sources for other media, so it is important to look closely at what was published about martial arts during the 1960s, 1970s, and 1980s. It seems that a large percentage of books and articles dealing with Asian martial traditions lacked true substance. Content was often biased, fueled by ego, or produced for profit and promotion. Texts included many inaccuracies and rarely included any references. Primary sources in Asian languages could be found in a few theses and dissertations, but these were rare occurrences since academia placed little importance on the Asian martial arts as a subject of study. Studies worth mentioning were those scientific articles about martial arts that fell in the areas of health and sports.

Donn Draeger's works stand out in their sincerity and accuracy, derived from solid scholarship and field research. *Asian Fighting Arts* (1969), coauthored with Robert W. Smith, is still in print and used for reference. A number of other books bearing Draeger's name as author also remain strong reference works. By contrast, dozens of books and hundreds of articles were produced by people who lacked qualifications—usually not being familiar with the cultural milieu where the arts developed, often in martial training itself, and sometimes in both of these areas. If a study were done of the published articles and books over these decades, the gems of quality writings would be few and far between.

By 1990, trends in publishing continued, producing more in quantity, but still lacking in quality. A few people tried to raise the standards by publishing periodicals, including *Judo Illustrated* under the hand of Donn Draeger, Hunter Armstrong's *Hoplos*, and Wayne Muromoto's *Fuyru* magazine. All had excellent quality, but were short lived and had limited influence. Plus, the focus remained on the Japanese arts.

If quality materials dealing with Japanese martial arts were scarce, materials dealing with Chinese arts were more so. Those wishing to gather information about martial traditions from other Asian countries were in a similar predicament. As any serious martial arts practitioner of that time knows, the personal collection of books and articles was inspiring, but not very reliable. And articles in foreign Asian script may have looked important, albeit incomprehensible without the language skills to translate.

Over the years, my interests in Asian culture deepened, academically as well as in the practical side of combatives. This background helped me to look at the martial arts as living traditions that were vital aspects within the cultures where they developed. Sadly, it became more and more apparent how shallow the representation of Asian martial traditions had been in the bulk of mass media. After graduating from the university, I decided to pursue work that I would enjoy and chose to start a serious journal on Asian martial arts. This would combine my academic studies, foreign travel experience, and favorite hobby.

Setting Goals for the *Journal of Asian Martial Arts*

I enjoyed studying martial arts and also learning about Asian culture. I wanted to go beyond the tournament circuits and *Teenage Mutant Ninja Turtles* (1987). Fiction and fantasy are fine for what they represent, but what was the reality of martial arts practice in Asia? What skills does a true master embody? How and why were the various martial arts developed? There simply was no reliable source that could provide such information. If a journal could be produced, perhaps it would attract qualified writers who would be inspired to contribute by sharing their knowledge and experiences.

The desire to produce a martial arts periodical led to many questions on how to organize it and set editorial goals. The initial vision was simply to provide what had been missing with most publications on the subject: reliable articles about Asian martial traditions. Authors had to be highly skilled in the martial art they wrote about, and preferably had a solid comprehension of the associated culture. The ideal would be to publish articles by knowledgeable, experienced scholar-practitioners. I set out to find people who fit this description. It was like hunting for the elusive unicorn, and some were found!

Standard academic journals served as guides. What were the authors' qualifications? Detailed bios had to be given. Where did the writers get their information? Authors had to provide their references and bibliographies so others could refer to them for reliability. Such guidelines were helpful, but I didn't want to totally limit the journal's readership to a dozen specialists, as many academic journals do. If produced solely for scholars, the articles would not be of much use for the vast majority of readers. It seemed best to keep the writing clear and readable, in plain, college-level English. Writers were asked to put foreign terms in brackets and be sure to provide definitions for any specialized terminology.

For a few millennia, China was a source of inspiration for neighboring peoples. All aspects of Chinese culture, such as medicine, architecture, and arts and crafts, were adapted by these bordering states. The martial arts were not an exception, and the Chinese influence can easily be seen in nearby Korea, Japan, and Southeast Asia, for example. Because of

China's profound influence, it was natural that Chinese martial traditions should be included in every journal.

Japanese martial arts were popular, plus they have a wonderful tradition of preservation through unbroken lines of instruction and solid historic documentation. We decided each journal should include at least one article about Japan.

What of the other areas and their unique martial art heritage? Kalaripayattu. Bando. Silat. . . . Hundreds of styles had names that were not yet well known in the West. Few could write about these rare styles. Some who pioneered studies in these lesser-known areas were born in European countries that had established long political relationships in Asia. For example, the Dutch wrote about the indigenous fighting arts of Indonesia, the French about Vietnamese fighting arts, and the British about Indian arts. Obtaining new articles on these lesser-known arts was difficult.

The search for qualified authors included writing letters to scholarly and martial art organizations, as well as to individual scholars and practitioners. A number of references were utilized, such as directories for Asian specialists and martial artists. From those contacted, some responded to the solicitation for articles.

The journal's title was selected and submissions were received. What next? Scholars from various areas of specialization were invited to participate with work on the journal and an editorial board was formed. Members would be helpful to review submissions, fact-check, edit, proof, and hopefully help bring in article submissions due to their professional contacts. Editorial guidelines were developed.

Next came the actual design of the physical journal: page size, type, layouts, logo, etc. Finding a printer was easy enough. Materials also had to be submitted to distributors with hopes to get journals into bookstores. We eventually worked with more than a dozen distributors that delivered the journal to all the major bookstore chains and many independent bookstores throughout the U.S. and Canada, plus some distribution to other foreign countries in Europe and Asia. The graphic elements from the journal design facilitated designing our first website.

Starting Via Media Publishing Company

All the plans to start the physical journal were made, but an actual business also needed to be legally founded. How to do this without much experience in publishing, and without financial backing? A company name was chosen in order to produce the periodical: Via Media Publishing. The name has overtones of Asian philosophy, since *via* means "way, path, or road," and *media* is the "middle" or what comes in between. A cost-effective location was soon found: my parents' attic!

The *Journal of Asian Martial Arts* was founded in 1991 with a long list of objectives for improving the quality of scholarship in this field, as well as raising the standards regarding actual practice. Via Media Publishing Company was embedded in the family home. The attic was the main office, with file cabinets, typewriter, and a newfangled thing called a computer—my first Macintosh, with which I could magically "cut and paste." The kitchen table served as the place to take phone orders, equipped with a charge card machine and record books. The dining room and living room became the shipping department for mailings every three months when a new journal was printed. Journals were stored in the basement and boxed or placed in padded mailers for any orders that came in between bulk mailings. Via Media didn't have digital products: the internet was starting to expand, but wasn't commercialized until 1995.

We prepared the house for work and prepared computer files and artwork for press. What were needed were orders. Over twenty thousand tri-fold announcements were mailed to martial art schools, libraries, and academic departments associated with Asian studies. The flyer included a postcard with the journal logo, details about the journal, and ordering information. I told my mom that perhaps we should put a big cardboard box under the regular mailbox to handle the response from the mass mailing. We waited daily in anticipation, but found we never needed an extra box.

Realities of Publishing the *Journal of Asian Martial Arts*

Our goal was to publish a serious periodical about Asian martial arts according to scholarly standards. This had never been successfully done before. After all was set in motion for publishing—journal design, article submissions, editing, printing, distribution, business organization—how would the journal be accepted?

When the journal was first announced in 1992, regular practitioners thought it sounded too scholarly and weren't interested. Academicians thought the subject not worthy to consider reading or including in a library. Whenever practitioners did see an issue, they found that it included techniques they could learn. When academics somehow opened the pages, they were surprised to see the scholarly articles were of high standard. The journal mixed heavier academic pieces with others of lighter reading. The number of subscribers slowly grew.

Scholarly tools are necessary in order to accurately present the martial arts. Each area of academic specialization can contribute to a clearer picture and understanding of this subject. We welcomed approaches from all academic disciplines: anthropology, history, linguistics, economics, philosophy, literature, law, physical education, sociology, etc. However, academic studies alone cannot fully present all aspects of the combative arts. Martial art masters were often illiterate, which does not detract from their great skills and insights. Reports, interviews, reflections, and "how to" articles are vital for understanding combat traditions. There were hundreds of article submissions, and each was considered for publication on its own merits.

We hoped that the quality and quantity of article submissions would improve with time by attracting writers who wanted to help improve the field with their experience and knowledge. Articles could inspire others to expand upon published pieces, follow up with further research, and bring new knowledge and insights to readers. People could collaborate, bringing individual talents and skills together to offer what no one single author could do alone.

As work began on each upcoming issue, we always worried that there would not be enough good material to fill it. As mentioned, most articles were rejected due to poor writing and research. It is easy to tell when an article is submitted as a promotion piece, an attempt to sell a product or service. A good number of academic-style articles looked scholarly, but didn't possess content worth publishing. Some scholarly articles were excellent, but only a few people could comprehend or benefit from the presentations. The long-joked-about formula "KISS: keep it simple, scholar," is unfortunately ignored by most who need to think about the real purpose of writing. Who are they writing for? Sometimes the more educated people become, the more they equate the use of foreign terms, specialized vocabulary, and complex sentence structure as their claim for being an authority. Ironically, many highly educated scholars were not smart enough to know how to write clearly for those outside their clique.

Dress like a samurai and you can take on the aura. Does writing with a mix of Japanese and English make one sound more educated? Some writers insisted on using Japanese terms according to Japanese usage. For example, "I practice kata." Is kata here singular or plural? In Japanese it is both, but not in English. Our journal was in English. The word kata has been absorbed into English and the plural is katas. However, to a westerner who has spent years trying to live and speak as a Japanese, it just doesn't seem right using "katas" in an English sentence.

The journal also utilized pinyin romanization for Chinese. Accordingly, we would use Daoism, xingyi, and taijiquan rather than Taoism, hsing-i, or t'ai chi ch'uan. The journal utilized such styles for academic reasons, not because of some whim, personal preference, or habit. Many potential authors could not adapt.

One writer submitted an excellent, well-written article. The ideas were insightful and would have benefited many readers. For such important articles, we required that sources be given so readers would know where the author obtained the information and could also follow up if they wished. All authors rehash old material. Better authors learn from others' writings and experiences, analyze them, and build upon them. In this case, when I asked the author to provide sources—books, articles, personal communications, etc.—he simply replied: "But Mike, I am the authority!" Sorry, this isn't good enough. This guy may be an authority, but only because he built upon others' work.

When we published the article "People and Events of Taekwondo's Formative Years," by Dakin Burdick, a number of people who practiced Taekwondo were outraged. The article showed that this art actually was derived from Japanese styles, debunking the belief that the style was purely Korean. A famous instructor in the U.S. sent a facsimile to me stating, "Taekwondo is Korean." No proof. No references. Just his brief statement. Why should anyone believe him?

Another famous teacher submitted an article about taiji for publication. I had some drawings made for the front of the article. After she saw the publication, she was furious. "That illustration looks like a man!" she said. I thought, "Well, Ms. Prima Donna, it wasn't supposed to be you." She threatened me with a lawsuit. So much for the peaceful ways of taiji and character building.

There were other articles submitted by well-known practitioners. Some articles were written well enough, but they didn't offer anything new. A few authors wrote about their masters, how they became disciples, and how they inherited the system, but didn't provide any new insights or information for our readers. I wanted material that had not been published elsewhere, and that would at least offer something fresh.

If any submission had potential, I would offer some feedback and suggestions. This is the work of an editor-in-chief. When authors were willing to work together, the end result would be an improved article that exceeded the author's original quest in quality. Others were offended that anyone could make any suggestions at all. They were deities above questioning. A number of times I was physically challenged to fisticuffs for offering suggestions or rejecting articles. Threats rather than cooperation. Their martial art skills may have been tops, but their character left much to be desired. Perhaps something missing in their training in the dojo, or even in the nursery school sandbox?

For twenty years we worried about having enough quality material for each issue. It would have been great to have enough material for two issues, so we could get ahead of schedule. That never happened.

Besides constantly worrying about article submissions, publishing requires much time to deal with production, distribution, advertising/promotion, orders, fulfillment, and to handle communications with subscribers. At one time we had a professional company handle advertising for the journal. Their work involved finding companies to purchase advertising space, receiving payments, and paying us after subtracting fees for their services. But they kept all the income! Clear robbery. Lawyers didn't want to pursue collection because there was not enough money in it for them. I eventually found one who would do it for the principal, won, and got paid. Others failed to pay for invoices, including advertisers, bookstores, distributors, and individuals.

Distributors paid whatever they wished. There was no way to know exactly how many journals sold through stores. Income varied greatly each quarter. As the world economy started to weaken, sometimes no payments were received from distributors. They paid bigger publishers, not smaller ones. Eventually, many distributors went bankrupt. Bookstores closed, including the Borders chain. In the end, many payments due Via Media remain unpaid.

Perhaps the biggest problem for us involved website design and maintenance, necessary for customer relations and providing products. Thousands of dollars were spent for promised services, especially in preparation for entering the digital age. Unfortunately, one company after another failed to provide the services agreed upon. So, the website always had problems. It was not userfriendly. Customers got frustrated, so many stopped trying to order products. Can't blame them.

During recent years there has been a decline in the quality of services proved in printing, distribution, fulfillment, and with website work. Costs are all increasing for less services. At the same time all costs were going up, our income decreased. In hard times, conventional wisdom says you stop any periodical subscriptions. Journal subscriptions slowed as expected. All other companies dealing with martial arts suffered as well. Enrollment in all martial art schools dwindled, and thousands of schools closed. Companies supplying products to these schools were forced into bankruptcy, to close, or at minimum to cut back. As part of the supply line, these companies could not afford to purchase advertising. Even the largest companies started to penny pinch.

I thought, maybe the economy will turn around. Maybe martial artists will want to delve deeper into the arts they practice. Leading martial arts scholars and practitioners will surely desire to help the journal improve by offering their input and quality articles. Now I think not in my lifetime. Twenty years of devotion to this field is enough, so we turned the last journal page. Others can carry on from here. Maybe I'll go sip tea in a bamboo grove.

Publishing Pleasures

As you can see from the preceding pages, there were many obstacles in publishing the journal. The fact that it was produced for twenty years indicates that there was some support: dedicated subscribers who never missed an issue, authors with a passion for research and commitment to enrich the field, long-time practitioners who generously shared their insights, and associate editors who helped polish articles into smooth reading. Unfortunately, the support was not enough to hold up a serious martial arts publication.

Alkimachon, a martial art publisher in Athens, published the *Journal of Asian Martial Arts* in Greek from 2006-2008. As a private company, the journal could not find enough support to continue. However, the University of León went full force into publishing a Spanish edition (*Revista de Artes Marciales Asiáticas*), starting in 2006. Since they have university support, their edition continues to this day.

For Via Media Publishing, beside the published articles, there is not much to show. No edifice for the company. No big list of awards or recognitions. However, it seems there were two great benefits. One is that producing the journal has been educational, covering all aspects of publishing, and primarily as an unique way to learn about martial traditions and their place in world history. The second and more important benefit is that this business served as a foyer where many strangers met, drawn by a common interest. Some became comrades in martial studies, and a smaller group became friends.

I have many memories of working with Robert W. Smith on Via Media's first book project: *Martial Musings: A Portrayal of Martial Arts in the 20th Century*. We had many conversations about martial arts and the colorful array of characters in this field, especially the self-proclaimed "masters." Smith's share of bitter experiences brought out his great wit and humor. He valued family over anything involving combatives, and that is a rare trait among martial art addicts.

I've also been blessed to personally meet with another luminary in this field, the late Oscar Ratti, a pioneer known for books he coauthored with his wife, Adele Westbrook. Oscar was not only the consummate martial scholar-practitioner, but a living renaissance man. His grasp of martial traditions, Eastern and Western, was extraordinary. His comprehension of martial traditions was thorough in both theory and application. He was so far ahead of his time that few could carry on a dialogue with him. The self-appointed leaders of martial studies were still doing basic addition and subtraction while Oscar was doing calculus. Physically formidable, this consistently polite man preferred seclusion to limelight. Despite being such a brilliant person, Oscar had a humble heart of gold that was filled with compassion for humankind. He didn't carry any of his great accomplishments on his sleeve, nor did he brag by waving the flag of ego. Signore Ratti was a rare gem in the martial arts world, and it was an honor to know him as a friend.

A fitting way to celebrate the end of the *Journal of Asian Martial Arts* was to produce a book: *Asian Martial Arts – Constructive Thoughts and Practical Applications*. It was result of friendships built during the double-decade life of the journal. Everyone who participated in this production did so out of friendship and a dedication to the spirit of the journal. These brothers- and sisters-in-arms answered a call without hesitation, all agreeing immediately to contribute. I admire all for their academic astuteness in this area of study and for their mastery of combative skills. In addition, I feel they represent a great group of respectful characters!

Finale

Both the successes and failures of the journal affected many involved in combative arts. If looked at closely, this publishing experience offers insights into the present state of Asian martial arts research and practice, and can benefit future endeavors in this field.

The original vision for the journal naively set goals that were impossible to achieve. That's clear to state now, but it wasn't two decades ago. We simply gave it our best effort and progress was made. The journal set an example for how academic tools could be applied in the field, such as incorporating standards in objectivity, linguistics, and referencing. As a result, there is certainly a stronger drive today to utilize a scholarly approach in writings dealing with martial traditions. In response, other periodical and book publishers raised their standards.

Rather than feature "how to" punch and kick articles, we strived to provide an editorial mix that enriched the combative side of Asian culture. Whenever you deal with true fighting arts, aspects of religion and medicine are naturally affiliated. Among any thinking hominids, ethical questions arise, including who should be taught lethal arts, and what are the responsibilities of both teachers and students. Without reflection and self-cultivation, we are doomed to suffer the consequences of failing to consider the seriousness of combatives as a part of the culture in which we live. Leaders in this field have a responsibility for the role martial art activities play in society, particularly as seen in acts of violence.

As vital cultural threads, the various martial arts have added color to every individual Asian milieu. Plus, like wet ink, they have stained others through cultural contacts. We are fortunate today that a number of fine scholars from all academic disciplines are applying their expertise to the study of martial traditions. The journal has introduced many of these scholars to its readers through their articles. Journal work has also introduced some scholars to each other, stimulating individual and collaborative efforts found in other publications and film documentaries.

Considering the journal's accomplishments as presented above, we know that they are just baby steps in the long trek toward what can still be accomplished in this field. For example, linguists should offer standard guidelines for romanization and provide clear definitions for related terminology. Weaponry and martial systems could be classified according to time and place. Writers can build upon previously published journal articles, verifying, expanding, and filling in missing areas of research.

Perhaps the most important part of martial arts scholarly research lies not in academia itself, but in the actual practice of these arts today and in the future. Why should people practice these arts in the first place? The answer will certainly include aspects of self-defense, law enforcement, artistic expression, sport, physical exercise, and therapy. Some instructors say they teach for health, but they often lack knowledge in basic human anatomy and kinetics. Many teach for self-defense, but their techniques may prove useless on the street. Olympic trainers focus on developing athletes, and often fail to incorporate new scientific studies to help their students. All of these martially-inspired expressions can benefit from scholarly studies, and hint at the enormous work that awaits for the serious scholar-practitioner.

Sorry to admit, but progress in this field will continue to be hindered by apathy, superficiality, super egos, jealousy, and uncooperativeness. I've been surprised that, after twenty years, the journal's main goals were not even understood by most associate editors. I hope that others more capable than I will be able to make solid advances in this field. Universities could support a martial arts publication. Scholarly conferences can either include panels on Asian martial arts, or be the sole focus for conferences. Books and articles by qualified individuals and coauthors will no doubt continue to be a growing influence.

What influence will martial arts play in our future? Some say they have no interest in the martial arts because combatives are strongly associated with violence. True, but although we do not like cancer, we certainly hope that some are studying it seriously. Likewise for the martial traditions, which are vital, evolving aspects of our human cultural tapestry. As such, we should not let the fighting arts spread haphazardly under the whims of ego, profit, and the primal release of violent instincts.

Unlike most physical activities, especially those associated with sports and recreation, the martial arts stand out for their potential to harm, maim, and kill. Just how these arts develop in the following decades will be determined by those having the most influence in sociopolitical affairs. Will they fail to take these arts seriously, as they have done with other cultural elements? Or will they become more responsible in handling this double-edged sword?

* This chapter was previously published in *Asian Martial Arts: Constructive Thoughts and Practical Application*, Santa Fe, NM: Via Media Publishing, pp. 154-167.

Chapter IV

The Journal of Asian Martial Arts: Content and Comments

Introduction

The following pages provide a list of all the articles published in the *Journal of Asian Martial Arts* from 1992 to 2016. The list follows an annual timeline for the journal and includes some highlights that occurred as a result of Via Media Publishing's place in martial arts publishing history.

From the list of 484 articles, you will find topics associated with specific geographic locations—Chinese gongfu, Japanese budo, Korean and Southeast Asian arts, and other areas. Topics may apply to many of the arts, regardless of origin, such a common techniques and body mechanics. On the academic side, a goal for the journal was to include articles that reach beyond physical techniques into all scholarly disciplines.

When I founded the journal, I thought many academic writers would be specialists with degrees in Asian Studies. It was a surprise that many had backgrounds in anthropology. Others came to submit articles from other disciplines, including psychology, sociology, history, politics, art, religion/philosophy, and economy. On one panel focusing on martial arts at an academic conference, I thought it strange that one professor's topic dealt with martial arts and hormones. Not a common topic, but his paper made total sense.

The martial arts are part of the cultural fabric in which they arose. Why are martial arts important to study? What effect does popular media play on martial art studies? We talk much about learning for self-defense, competition, and health. There are other reasons. Those of a violent nature may have a natural inclination to learn the most lethal methods. Some study martial arts for their aesthetic beauty and dance-like qualities.

One value of reading the article list is to see how the topics changed over the decades. When did MMA topics enter the list? What research has been done that provides information not available previously? What authors were inspired by reading a journal article and wrote a follow up piece? Have any of the authors collaborated to submit an article for publication? The authors published were not just from the U.S.A. and

Canada, but from Europe, Central and South America, and Asia as well.

In addition to the articles, journals include reviews of books, DVDs, videos, and movies. Some excellent poetry was published too. These are not listed here.

For over two decades the *Journal of Asian Martial Arts* was a serious forum for authors to present their finest works on a variety of martial topics. Most articles included useful bibliographies to support statements and conclusions. Often the articles would lead to more questioning. As a periodical, the journal was a start of serious inquiry into martial traditions. There is still much more to do. Hopefully the articles here will inspire future work and publications, expanding on the breath of topics and the depth of research.

ARTICLES IN THE JOURNAL OF ASIAN MARTIAL ARTS
——————— 1992 ———————

Volume 1 • Number 1
- STUBENBAUM, D. Wu Kuang-hsien: A traditional look at martial art practice.
- DeMarco, M. The origin and evolution of taijiquan.
- Wong, J. A brief description of Chen style master Du Yutse (M. DeMarco, Trans.).
- ZARRILLI, P. To heal and/or harm: The vital spots (*marmmam/varmam*) in two south Indian martial traditions, part I: Focus on Kerala's kalarippayattu.
- JONES, D. Testing for shodan in Japan: Kyudo and jyodo.
- PIETER, W. AND TAAFFE, D. The Oregon taekwondo research project: Results and recommendations.
- DONOHUE, J. Dancing in the danger zone: The martial arts in America.
- DeMarco, M. Glimpsing martial traditions in the Cleveland museum of art.

Volume 1 • Number 2
- ZARRILLI, P. To heal and/or harm: The vital spots (*marmmam/varmam*) in two south Indian martial traditions, part II: Focus on the Tamil art of varma ati.
- MALISZEWSKI, M. Injuries and effects of martial arts: A review.
- MALISZEWSKI, M. Medical, healing and spiritual components of Asian martial arts: A preliminary field study exploration.
- DRENGSON, A. Aikido: Its philosophy and application.
- SECKLER, J. Swordsmanship and neo-Confucianism: The tengu's art.
- DONOHUE, J. A sort of swordsman (fiction).

Volume 1 • Number 3 • Special Issue
- MALISZEWSKI, M. Meditative-religious traditions of fighting arts and martial ways.

Volume 1 • Number 4
- SPIESSBACH, M. Bodhidharma: Meditating monk, martial arts master or make-believe?
- CRAWFORD, A. The martial yen: American participation in the aikido tradition.
- NEMETH, D. Comment: Neo-Confucianism and the east Asian martial arts.
- IMAMURA, H. AND NAKAZAWA, A. Philosophy and history of Japanese martial arts: Idealism or pragmatism?
- HOLCOMBE, C. Theater of combat: A critical look at the Chinese martial arts.
- DELZA, S. The presence of the eyes in the action of taijiquan.
- LAURENT, D. Laws of change or seeing the unseen in martial arts.
- MANYAK, A. AND SILVAN, J. The material culture of the martial arts: Exhibiting Okinawan karate.

Comments

"A journey of 10,000 miles begins with the first step." Once the decision was made to publish the first issue of the *Journal of Asian Martial Arts*, there was no turning back. A prerequisite was letting potential authors know we were looking for article submissions. In accord with the journal logo—a symbolic fusion of sword and pen tips—martial art scholar/practitioners responded.

The four issues in Volume 1 contained 22 articles. As expected, most of these focused on Chinese and Japanese martial traditions, with others on taekwondo, and two arts from south India. Of major importance is the inclusion of academic articles dealing with topics of sociology, medical aspects and philosophy.

Four members of the Editorial Board contributed to the first volume. Most notable were articles by Dr. Michael Maliszewski and the special issue, Volume 1 Number 3: Meditative-Religious Traditions of Fighting Arts and Martial Ways. His years of studying martial traditions, including field research in many Asian locations—including countries as Indonesia and Tibet—is apparent in this excellent work. We published this along with his extensive bibliography. An abridged version was later published by Tuttle as *Spiritual Dimensions of the Martial Arts*.

As a new periodical, the *Journal of Asian Martial Arts* was selected as "One of the Ten Best Magazines of 1991" by the Council of Editors of Learned Journals.

Volume 2 • Number 1
- HOLCOMBE, C. The Daoist origins of the Chinese martial arts.
- PIETER, W. European and Japanese medieval warriors.
- DONOHUE, J. Social organization and martial systems: A cross-cultural typology.
- LOWRY, D. Non-Asian combative arts: An informal hoplological inquiry.
- LEHRHAUPT, L. Taijiquan: Learning how to learn.
- EISEN, M. Gin-foon Mark: Classical versus modern gongfu.
- SHINE, J. Sohei: The warrior monks of old Japan.
- HOSHINO, H. Bladed weaponry with illustrations from the Japanese Antique Sword Museum.

1993 Volume 2 • Number 2
- WILSON, J. Chasing the magic: Mysticism and the martial arts on the island of Java.
- YOUNG, R. The history and development of taekyon.
- MASSEY, P., ET AL. Increased lung capacity through qigong breathing techniques of the Chung Moo martial art style.
- PEGG, R. Master Sun's the *Art of War*.
- PEPPER, S. The martial arts: Rites of passage, dramas of persuasion.
- DEMARCO, M. Glimpsing martial traditions in the Johnson-Humrickhouse Museum.

1993 Volume 2 • Number 3
- WINGATE, C. Exploring our roots: Historical and cultural foundations of ideology of karate-do.
- TAYLOR, K. The history of iaido: A Japanese sword art.
- DERRICKSON, C. Thoughts on the *Classic of Taijiquan*.
- STEIN, J. Art and the martial artist.
- BOLZ, M. Three distinctive techniques of Pwang Gai Noon Ryu.
- STEBBINS, J. The makiwara as a tool for learning.
- SUTTON, N. Gongfu, guoshu, and wushu: State appropriation of the martial arts in modern China.

1992 Volume 2 • Number 4
- PIETER, W. Body & mind in medieval and pre-modern Japanese martial arts.
- BATES, C. An excerpt from *Tales of Chivalrous and Altruistic Heros*: 'Wang Wu notices the commotion of music hall street'.

- HURST, G. From heiho to bugei: The emergence of the martial arts in Tokugawa Japan.
- STEBBINS, J. The functional anatomy of the hip for martial arts.
- BARLOW, J. AND DAY, M. Ethnic strife and the origins of kajukenbo.
- WILEY, M. Silat seni gayong: Seven levels of defense.
- MAGNUSON, J. The dancing taiji masters.

Comments

In Volume 2, there were a good variety of topics presented in 28 articles. Most focused on Chinese and Japanese martial tradition. Others were on Korean and Southeast Asian arts, and martially-related items in the Johnson-Humrickhouse Museum. Popular topics included taijiquan and karate and rarer arts as Kajukenbo, Silat Seni Gayong, plus specific styles as Pwang Gai Noon Ryu.

The scholarly perspectives are seen in articles dealing with functional anatomy, methods for classifying martial arts, and comparative studies as in Pieter's look at Japanese and European medieval warriors. A number of the authors dove deeply into the history and cultures which nourished the martial traditions in their articles. For example, Dr. Hurst's piece stands out as only a Japan scholar could present the details of martial arts as living elements in the Tokugawa period (1603–1867). Dr. Holcombe brought forth the presence of Daoism in China's martial evolution. James Wilson showed how strong mysticism gives flavor for Indonesian silat.

As ocurred in a the previous volume, Volume 2 included an article that caught the editorial eye of a book publishing house. Shambhala Publications liked the article by Linda Lehrhaupt on "Taijiquan—Learning How to Learn." Via Media helped it to be published by Shambhala as *T'ai Chi as a Path of Wisdom*.

Work on the *Journal of Asian Martial Arts* had some recognition in 1993 as I was inducted into the World Martial Arts Hall of Fame as founder of the periodical.

———— 1994 ————

Volume 3 • Number 1
- DONOHUE, J. Wave people: The martial arts and the American imagination.
- PERITZ, C. The Ainu and their swords in Japan: A concise overview.
- BALDWIN, F. The game of go and the martial arts
- SUTTON, N. The development of Zheng Manqing [Cheng Man-ch'ing] taijiquan in Malaysia.

- MONDAY, N. The ryu ha system: Continuity and change in Japanese martial culture.
- PIETER, W. Notes on the historical development of Korean martial sports—An addendum to Young's history and development of taekyon.
- STUBENBAUM, D. An encounter with Chen Xiaowang: The continuing development of Chen style taijiquan.

Volume 3 • Number 2
- PIETER, W. Research in martial sports: A review.
- AMDUR, E. Divine transmission Katori Shinto Ryu.
- DELLA PIA, J. Korea's *Muye Dobo Tongji*.
- WILEY, M. Classical eskrima: The evolution and etymology of a Filipino fencing form.
- McCARTHY, P. The world within Kinjo Hiroshi and karatedo.

Volume 3 • Number 3
- ZARRILLI, P. Actualizing power(s) and crafting a self in kalarippayattu: A south Indian martial art and the yoga and ayurvedic paradigms.
- HERSHEY, L. Shotokan karate as non-discursive intercultural exchange.
- PORTA, J. AND McCABE, J. The karate of Chojun Miyagi.
- YOKOYAMA, K. The sources of power in karate.
- SUINO, K. How to watch iaido.
- DeMARCO, M. The necessity for softness in taijiquan.

Volume 3 • Number 4
- DONOHUE, J. AND TAYLOR, K. The classification of the fighting arts.
- WILEY, M. Silat kebatinan as an expression of mysticism and martial culture in Southeast Asia.
- FRIMAN, H. AND POLLAND, R. Striving for realism: Concerns common to martial arts and law enforcement training.
- STUBENBAUM, D. AND BRINKMAN, M. Some insights into xingyi quan: Interview with Lo Dexiu.
- TAYLOR, K. Use of the knife and short staff in aikido training.
- SHINE, J. *Honcho bugei shoden*: The original martial arts survey.

Comments

In the third year publishing the journal, articles were particularly strong on topics dealing with Japan. Eleven focused on Japan, followed by 4 on China, 2 on Korea, and 1 each on Southeast Asian and India. Dr. John Donohue hits home with martial arts in America as a social phenomenon. Friman and Polland present aspects of martial arts as utilized for law enforcement—a hot topic today.

Article topics spread beyond the norm to include aikido, xingyiquan, and weapons, such as the knife and staff. Ellis Amdur provided an encompassing coverage of Katori Shinto Ryu. An example of collaboration that happened with the journal's influence is when Donohue and Taylor—two Associate Editors for the journal—joined forced to present methodologies for classification of the fighting arts. John Della Pia's analysis of Korea's *Illustrated Manual of Martial Arts* (*Muye Dobo Tongji*, originally compiled in 1790), added to his qualifications for black belt promotion.

Fredric Baldwin brought an exciting read on how the game of Go embodies a martial art spirit. Another joy to read was Curtis Peritz's work on "The Ainu and their swords in Japan." Decades of research are evident in his article. With his focus on the indigenous people of northern Japan, not only shared the unique Ainu culture and their sword tradition, but how they related to the Japanese culture too.

———— **1995** ————

Volume 4 • Number 1
- FLORENCE, R. The importance of romanizing Chinese martial art terms.
- AMDUR, E. The development and history of the naginata.
- SMITH, R.W. Zheng Manqing (Cheng Man-ch'ing) and taijiquan: A clarification of role.
- ZARRILLI, P. The kalarippayattu martial master as healer: Traditional Kerala massage therapies.
- BOLZ, M. The Okinawan sai: A kobudo weapon for self-defense.

Volume 4 • Number 2
- ROSENBERG, D. Paradox and dilemma: The martial arts and American violence.
- NEIDE, J. Martial arts and Japanese nationalism.
- HOYT, S. Martial arts behind the Berlin wall.
- DAVEY, H. The history and legacy of Japan's *Kokusai Budoin*.
- LIM, T. Principles and practices in taijiquan.
- KOHLER, S. Inner circle taiji training exercises.
- DELLA PIA, J. Native Korean sword techniques described in the *Muye Dobo Tongji*.

Volume 4 • Number 3
- AMDUR, E. Maniwa nen-ryu.
- PAUKA, K. The pauleh tinggi ceremony in West Sumatra.
- SMITH, R. W. Remembering Zheng Manqing [Cheng Man-ch'ing]: Some sketches from his life.
- WILEY, M. An interview with Hou Faxiang concerning qigong practice.
- WOLFE, R. Control of center: The technical, strategic, and spiritual foundations of ko-ryu karate-do.

Volume 4 • Number 4
- VARLEY, P. Samurai in school: Ryuha in traditional Japanese martial arts.
- HURST, G. Ryuha in the martial and other Japanese arts.
- FRIDAY, K. Kabala in motion: Kata and pattern practice in the traditional bugei.
- HESSELINK, R. The warrior's prayer: Tokugawa Yoshimune revives the yabusame ceremony.
- BOUDREAU, F., ET. AL. Psychological and physical changes in school-age karate participants: Parental observations.
- CHAUDHURI, J. Defending the motherline: Wing chun's sil lum tao.
- PARKER, C. Opening and closing: An introduction to the welcoming postures of pencak silat.

Comments

    Articles in Volume 4 continues with a balanced coverage of geographic areas: Japan 11, China 7, Korea 1, Southeast Asia 2, and India 1. Contributions from Roberts W. Smith on Zheng Manqing added to the understanding of this particular branch of taijiquan. Articles on Chinese qigong and south Indian massage illustrate these modalities for maintaining or regaining health. Dr. Pauka's unique field work brought the pauleh tinggi ceremony to our eyes. This rare three-day long event brings together silat performances by individuals, pairs, and groups that go on throughout each day and night.

    For weapons, Mary Bolz brings her experience from Okinawa on practical use of the sai. Ellis Amdur provides wonderful coverage on the history and use of the naginata. Academic topics covered the effects on children studying martial arts, the relationship between martial arts and violence in America, and Richard Florence's article on the importance of romanizing Chinese martial art terms.

    As a bonus, Volume 4 Number 4 included papers presented at the Association for Asian Studies Annual Meeting, 1993. The head of the pannel was Dr. Paul Varley, emeritus professor at Columbia University and Sen Soshitsu XV Professor of Japanese Cultural History at the University of Hawaii. As he notes: "The following papers bring together for the first time, to my knowledge, a group of scholars specializing in Japanese history, who are also practitioners of the martial arts, to present studies on aspects of these arts." Here, the articles by Hurst, Friday and Hesselink dive deeply into Japanese history and culture, providing a Japanese perspective on the martial traditions, in contrast to the often fanciful perspective in the West. Of particular interest here is the piece by Dr. Hesselink on mounted archery.

——————— **1996** ———————

Volume 5 • Number 1
- NG, W.M. The *Yi Jing* in the military thought of Tokugawa Japan.
- SMITH, R.W. Han Qingtang and his seizing art.
- WATSON, C. Spiritual versus martial aikido: Explanation and reconciliation.
- HOLT, R. Shoto Tanemura discusses the roots of modern ninpo.
- TAYLOR, J. An interview with Brian Frost on the practice of tameshiwari.
- DURSTINE, L. AND NETHERTON, B. Warming-up for martial arts practice: Scientific foundations.
- DAVEY, H. Donn Draeger and the international hoplology society.

Volume 5 • Number 2
- AMDUR, E. The role of arms-bearing women in Japanese history.
- DAVIS, B. In search of a unified dao: Zheng Manqing's life and contribution to taijiquan.
- PORTA, J. AND McCABE, J. Supplementary weight training for Miyagi Chojun's Goju-ryu karate.
- TYREY, B. AND BRINKMAN, M. The luo-shu as taiji boxing's secret inner-sanctum training method.
- TAYLOR, K. AND OHMI, G. An interview with Japanese sword instructor Haruna Matsuo.
- PHELPS, S. The unique legacy of wu-dang master Fu Zhensong.

Volume 5 • Number 3
- FRIMAN, H. Blinded by the light: Politics and profit in the martial arts.
- WILEY, M. The classification and ethos of Filipino martial traditions.
- FREUND, R. Karate techniques: Applied physiology and biomechanics.
- LEVITT, E. Fit to print: Martial arts as covered in major American newspapers.

- POLYAKOV, L., ET AL. The variety of submission holds developed and applied by leading sambo practitioners.
- SMITH, R. The masters contest of 1926: An epiphany in judo history.
- FLORENCE, R. An interview with Uehara Seikichi on Motobu-ryu udun-di bujutsu.
- LIM, T. The combative elements of Yang Taijiquan.
- MANCUSO, T. Stillness in the martial arts.

Volume 5 • Number 4
- VAN HORNE, W. Ideal teaching: Japanese culture and the training of the warrior.
- SMITH, R.W. Breathing in taiji and other fighting arts.
- DAVIS, D. AND MANN, L. Conservator of the taiji classics: An interview with Benjamin Pang Jeng Lo.
- PHELPS, S. Gift of the shorinjin: The art of shorinjin-ryu Saito ninjitsu.
- DEMARCO, M. Martial themes on Kang Xi porcelains in the Taft Museum.

Comments

Twenty-seven articles were published in Volume 5, most on China and Japan topics, 1 on Filipino martial arts. The practical articles focused on aspects such as breaking (*tameshiwari*) and joint locking (*qinna*), and more subtle tie-in practices of breathing, stilling the mind, warm-up exercise, and weight training. The variety of topics ranged from specific karate systems (Goju-ryu and Motobu-ryu), to Russian Sambo, Japanese Ninpo, Saito Ninjitsu, and Chinese taiji. Unusual topics appeared too: martial arts as reported in newspapers, and politics and profit in martial arts. Ellis Amdur offered another important study on the role of arms-bearing women in Japanese history.

Outstanding in this year's publications were articles with highly detailed presentations of specific systems and their leading representatives. Taylor interviewed Japanese sword instructor Haruna Matsuo. Barb Davis utilized decades of research to present Zheng Manqing's life and contribution to taijiquan. Somehow Davis and Mann wrote a thorough coverage of Benjamin Pang Jeng Lo, a taiji disciple of Zheng Manqing who rarely gave interviews. Years in Okinawa allowed Richard Florence to produce the highly detailed article on Uehara Seikichi and his style of Motobu-ryu. Shannon Phelps wrote of Mark Saito and the style of Shorinjin-ryu Ninjitsu from the Saito clan of Fukushima, Japan. These articles provided information and insights not previously available.

1997

Volume 6 • Number 1
- WILLMONT, D. Sacrifice, ritual, and alchemy: The spiritual traditions in taijiquan.
- BURDICK, D. People and events in taekwondo's formative years.
- SMITH, R.W. Chen Weiming, Zheng Manqing [Cheng Man-ch'ing] and the difference between strength and intrinsic energy.
- PAUKA, K. Silek: The martial arts of the Minangkabau in West Sumatra.
- TAYLOR, K. AND OHMI, G. The Omori-ryu: A history and explanation.

Volume 6 • Number 2
- DONOHUE, J. Ideological elasticity: Enduring form and changing function in the Japanese martial tradition.
- SIEG, B. How Western perceptions influenced the martial arts in old Shanghai.
- PITTMAN, A. William E. Fairbairn: British pioneer in Asian martial arts.
- SMITH, R.W. Da lu and some tigers.
- DOWD, S. Showing the forms of Filipino kuntaw lima-lima.
- HENDREY, E. Viewing human conflict through the martial arts: Interview with Dr. Terrance Webster-Doyle.
- FLORENCE, R. Ninth international seminar of budo culture.

Volume 6 • Number 3
- HENNING, S. Chinese boxing: The internal versus external schools in the light of history and theory.
- GALAS, M. Kindred spirits: The art of the sword in Germany and Japan.
- DEMARCO, M. Taijiquan as an experiential way for discovering Daoism.
- LORDEN, M. The distinguishing traits of Mas Oyama and Kyokushin karate.
- WOLFE, R. A method for teaching aerial breakfalls.
- POLLAND, R. Hikiotoshi uchi kihon: Jodo's pull and drop strike.
- WILEY, M. Philippine arms and armor in the University of Pennsylvania Museum of Archaeology and Anthropology.

Volume 6 • Number 4
- PAUKA, K. A flower of martial arts: The Randai folk theatre of the Minangkabau in West Sumatra.
- AMOS, D. A Hong Kong southern praying mantis cult.
- LONG, J. Jujutsu: The gentle art and the strenuous life.
- OUYANG, Y. The elevation of taekkyon from folk game to martial art.
- DONOHUE, J. The shape of water: Martial arts styles as technical continuum.

Comments

Along with China and Japan with 7 articles each, Volume 6 included 2 articles on Korea and 4 on Southeast Asia. Main styles discussed here are Kyokushin, taijiquan, taekwondo, southern mantis, taekkyon, silat, and Filipino kuntaw. Dakin Burdick's article, including solid historic documentation, shocked many in the claim that taekwondo is based on karate. Previously, many didn't have the facts to conclude this truth. The perception has since changed.

When I view the list of authors here, I'm reminded that one received photographs from an institute for use to illustrate his article. He was to pay for these rights, which he failed to do. Although talented and intelligent, his dishonesty became apparent in other cases besides this particular incident. I'm saddened by this, but the fine characters of so many others who submitted articles to the journal remain a blessing. Many highly skilled, brilliant contributors have remained friends over the next decades, including Robert Wolfe, Daniel Amos, Kirsten Pauka, and Richard Florence —all who contributed to Volume 6.

In the 29-page article "Sacrifice, ritual, and alchemy: The spiritual traditions in taijiquan," Dennis Willmont relied on his expertise in Chinese medicine and knowledge of Daoism. His scholarly presentation included the support of a fine reference list. I was working on the same topic, but had a simple presentation. Published six months later came "Taijiquan as an experiential way for discovering Daoism." An earlier version of this article was presented at the 73rd annual meeting of the Central States Anthropological Society in 1996, in Covington, KY.

Brand Sieg's article gives a lively account of martial arts as they appeared in "Old Shanghai" over a century ago. Since Shanghai had an international settlement, the mix of French, Indian, Russian, Japanese, British, American, and others fostered a unique hotbed for martial mixing. Allen Pittman's article fit well with this particular journal, Number 2.

Because of the journal work, I was invited to consult on a movie called *The Secrets of the Warrior's Power* (1997). It was a 44-minute documentary by Rising Sun Productions that appeared on the Discovery Channel.

———— 1998 ————

Volume 7 • Number 1
- PIETER, W. AND VAN RYSSEGEM, G. Serious injuries in karate and taekwondo.
- SVINTH, J. The school of hard knocks: Seattle's Kurosaka/Tentoku Kan Dojo 1928-1942.

- BINDER, B. AND COLEMAN, D. Applying taiji principles in Waboku Jujutsu.
- WALLACE, A. Internal training: The foundation for Chen Taiji's fighting skills and health promotion.
- HENNING, S. Reflections on a visit to the Shaolin Temple.

Volume 7 • Number 2
- BRESLOW, A. Immortality in Chinese thought and its influence on taijiquan and qigong.
- GROSSMAN, E. Toward a semiosis of the martial arts: Aikido as a symbolic form of communication.
- NIILER, T. Landing impact, loading, and injury risk to the lower legs in Chinese wushu.
- BLUMING, J. Without spirit budo is but an empty shell.
- GRADY, J. Celluloid katas: Martial arts in the movies: A practitioner's prejudices.

Volume 7 • Number 3
- FRIMAN, H. R. The art of regulation: Martial arts as threats to social order.
- HENNING, S. Southern fists and northern legs: The geography of Chinese boxing.
- SMITH, R. W. General Gao Fangxian and the vitality of northern Shaolin boxing.
- BOLZ, M. Kinjo Takashi Kaicho's advice to karateka: 'Use both hands!'
- MAINFORT, D. Chen and Yang Taiji converge in Hangzhou city.
- SILVAN, J. Oral traditions of Okinawan karate.

Volume 7 • Number 4
- O'CONNOR, M. Mind-body connections in Chen Xin's *Illustrated Explanation of Chen Style Taijiquan.*
- DEMARCO, M. Yang taiji practice through the eyes of Western medical health guidelines.
- SUENAKA, R. AND WATSON, C. Aikido kokyu-nage: The sublime and the practical.
- NONGMAITHEM, K. AND JIRGENSONS, K. Thang-ta: The martial art of Manipur India.
- PHELPS, S. One source, four images: Fu Yonghui's sixiang boxing.
- VAN HORNE, W. The history, principles and precepts of Sakugawa Koshiki Shorinji-ryu karate-do.

Comments

Volume 7 is particularly strong with 10 articles about China, followed by 8 for Japan and 1 each for Korea and India. Styles discussed included taekwondo, taijiquan, Shorinji-ryu, aikido, and an art from northern India called thang-ta. On the medical side, Pieter and Ryssegem's scholarly look at injuries occurring from karate and taekwondo is insightful reading for any martial art enthusiast. Timothy Niiler's article, "Landing impact, loading, and injury risk to the lower legs in Chinese wushu," is certainly helpful for understanding how to prevent leg injuries, especially in regards to jumping techniques. My own article outlines Western medical health guidelines for taijiquan practice, originally written to present at the 8th European Congress International Council for Health, Physical Education, Recreation, Sport and Dance held in London, England, in 1998.

One of the journals regular contributors was Robert W. Smith. In Number 3, he writes about "General Gao Fangxian and the vitality of northern Shaolin." Because of his influence, other writers submitted articles to the journal. One here is the famous karateka and judoka from Holland, Jon Bluming. In Number 2, you'll find his piece "Without spirit budo is but an empty shell." Another welcomed author was a student of R.W. Smith: James Grady, whose early novel *Six Days of the Condor* became a movie starring Robert Redford. Grady's fine work in this volume is titled "Celluloid katas: Martial arts in the movies—A practitioner's prejudices."

In 1998 a 96-minute documentary called *Mystic Origins of the Martial Arts* made a debut on A&E/History Channel. It is a Weller/Grossman Production. I participated as a consultant and appeared in a few segments. George Takei narrated.

——— **1999** ———

Volume 8 • Number 1
- Lohse, F. Self-transformation and the martial arts in the American cultural environment.
- Svinth, J. Masato Tamura, Ryoichi Iwakiri, and the Fife Judo Dojo, 1923-1942.
- Neide, J. Martial arts 101: Teaching at the college level.
- Ward, B. Energy projection in aikido wrist techniques.
- Pittman, A. Single palm change: Bagua's core movement.
- McKenna, M. Re-examining Ryukyu kobudo: An interview with Minowa Katsuhiko.
- Kohler, S. The nature of rooting in taijiquan: A survey.

Volume 8 • Number 2
- KLENS-BIGMAN, D. Toward a theory of martial arts as performance art.
- JACQUES, B. AND ANDERSON, S. The development of sambo in Europe and America.
- OLSON, G., COOK, M. AND BROOKS, L. Aikido's arm-lock (*ude-gatame*) technique: What tissues are affected?
- NOBLE, G. An introduction to W. Barton-Wright (1860-1951) and the eclectic art of bartitsu.
- CRAIG, K. Internal martial arts of Taiwan: An interview with Marcus Brinkman.
- LABBATE, M. Elements of advanced karate technique.

Volume 8 • Number 3
- HENNING, S. Chinese boxing's ironic odyssey.
- SMITH, R.W. Donn F. Draeger: A lifelong embodiment of the samurai code.
- DRAEGER, D. Letters on Miyamoto Musashi.
- FRIMAN, H. Donald F. Draeger's Wisconsin grave.
- BOWEN, R. Origins of the British Judo Association, the European Judo Union, and the International Judo Federation.
- WOLFE, R. The science of ukemi.
- PECK, A. The pedagogy of taijiquan in the university setting.
- ONDASH, A. Hung-Gar's ghost leg technique.

Volume 8 • Number 4
- AMOS, D. AND SUN, M. Spirit boxing in Hong Kong: Two observers, native and foreign.
- MCKENNA, M. An interview with Murakami Katsumi: The heart of Ryukyu's martial ways.
- PITTMAN, A. Combat wrestling: Geoghegan's blend from east to west.
- SVINTH, J. Ukiyo-e: Sumo as martial art.
- FIGLER, R., AND YANG, T. Bajiquan and piguazhang, pt. I: Foundational training methods.

Comments
There is 26 articles in Volume 8. As far as geographic areas covered, Japan has 12 articles, China 8, and 1 on Russian Sambo. Topics included bagua, karate, aikido, bajiquan, piguazhang, judo, wrestling, Ryukyu kobudo, and Hung Gar. Other articles are on topics of sumo in Japanese prints, teaching martials arts at college level, martial arts as a performance art, and pioneer Barton-Wright and his art of bartitsu.

Frederick Lohse's scholarly article, "Self-transformation and the martial arts in the American cultural environment," superbly covers important aspects for all martial artists. Through first-hand experience with *shenda* "spirit boxing" in Hong Kong, Amos and Sun share a rare window on a southern Chinese martial art as combined with mystical practices and involvement in secret societies. In their article, Jacques and Anderson cover "The development of sambo in Europe and America." Richard Bowen covers much on "Origins of the British Judo Association, the European Judo Union, and the International Judo Federation."

Besides being an internationally superstar as a practitioner in many Japanese martial arts, Donald Draeger (1922–1982) was an excellent writer of many books on combat arts. In Volume 8 Number 3, we had the fortune of posthumously publishing a short piece by him titled "Letters on Miyamoto Musashi." These letters were sent to his friend Robert W. Smith, who submitted them to the journal along with his wonderful account of his dear friend, titled: "Donn F. Draeger: A lifelong embodiment of the samurai code." Fittingly, Dr. Friman wrote a piece about locating and visiting Draeger's Wisconsin gravesite. Friman was accompanied by budo dignitaries Kaminoda Tsunemoru, Shimizu Takaji, and others.

--- 2000 ---

Volume 9 • Number 1
- HENNING, S. Traditional Korean martial arts.
- FIGLER, R., AND YANG, T. Bajiquan and Piguazhang, part II: Foundational training methods.
- LEVITAS, A. Ancient weapons for modern police.
- LABBATE, M. Developing advanced Goju-ryu techniques: Illustrated in the rising block.
- HAWTHOREN, M. Reviving the Daoist roots of internal martial arts.
- FLANAGAN, S. Use of the wrist in the vertical punch and the twisting straight punch.

Volume 9 • Number 2
- DEMARCO, M. The importance of martial arts research and practice.
- GREER, J. Swordsmanship and esoteric spirituality: An introduction to Gerard Thibault's Academie de l'Espee.
- DAVIES, P. What is kuntao? Cultural marginality in the Indo-Malay martial arts tradition.
- DEMARCO, M. AND MATTHEWS, A. The nurturing ways of Chen Taiji: An

interview with Yang Yang.
- SAKUYAMA, Y. Kon and haku: The spirit of heaven and earth in children.

Volume 9 • Number 3
- DYKHUIZEN, J. Culture, training, and perception of the martial arts: Aikido's example.
- MCKENNA, M. To-on-ryu: A glimpse into karate-do's roots.
- MCKENNA, M. Kanzaki Shigekazu: An interview with To-on-ryu's leading representative.
- MALISZEWSKI, M. Inside interview with Curtis Wong: Extraordinary contributions to martial arts popularization.
- MANCUSO, T. The web of breath: Weaving life's energy into your martial arts practice.
- EDWARDS, D. Character formulas in seven star praying mantis.

Volume 9 • Number 4
- DONOHUE, J. Sound and fury: Auditory elements in martial ritual.
- PAZ-Y-MIÑO, G. Predicting kumite strategies: A quantitative approach to karate.
- BABIN, R. Amateur saya craft: Scabbards in the making.
- GRADY, J. Fist of fantasy: Martial arts and prose fiction.
- TEDESCHI, M. Hapkido's defenses against multiple opponents.

Comments

Volume 9 includes 22 articles, 6 on Japan, 5 on China, 2 on Korea and 1 on Southeast Asia. Authors focused on a mix of styles, including aikido, Goju-ryu, To-on-ryu, Seven Star Praying Mantis, bajiquan, piguaquan, Chen Taiji, and kuntao of Indo-Malaysia. Other topics could embrace many martial art styles. Paz-y-mino's piece on predicting kumite strategies offers a scientific analysis of the possible options. On a finer point, another article looks closely into the kinetics of punching techniques. Tedeschi covers Hapkido's defenses against multiple opponents. Two articles were on weaponry, one being what ancient weapons are suitable for today's police work, and another on making scabbards. Ted Mancuso writes about breathing methods useful for martial artists, while Sakuyama presents nurturing ways for children, including their affinity for being in the open air spaces of nature.

Associate Editor Michael Maliszewski provides an in-depth interview with Curtis Wong—publisher of martial art magazines, books, and DVDs, in addition to being a skill martial artist and appeared in the TV *Kung Fu* series. Novelist James Grady makes an important contribution in line with his expertise: "Fist of fantasy: Martial arts and prose fiction." John Donohue's scholarly presentation of "Sound and fury: Auditory elements in martial ritual" makes readers think about this often overlooked part of martial traditions.

Ending the first decade of publishing the journal came with some blessings. One was being asked to consult and appear in a special two-hour documentary called *Martial Arts: The Real Story*. It was produced by Pacific Street Films and debuted on The Learning Channel. Working on the film in New York City was interesting and fun. A great joy came from the opportunity to meet some martial artists I only learned of through books or talked with by phone. Two key figures in the film were Robert W. Smith and Jon Bluming. Although Oscar Ratti was not involved with the documentary, I took the opportunity to introduce him for the first time to his contemporary Robert Smith—a great chat over lunch I won't forget.

Another wonderful memory for me was presenting the keynote address for the First World Congress on Fighting Sports and Martial Arts, 2000, in Amiens, France. This was published in Volume 9 Number 2 as "The importance of martial arts research and practice."

——————— 2001 ———————

Volume 10 • Number 1
- PARKER, P. The impact factor of the *Journal of Asian Martial Arts*.
- YAO, H. Martial-acrobatic arts in Peking Opera with a brief analysis of fighting movement in a scene from *The Three-Forked Crossroad*.
- MASON, R. Fifty years in the fighting arts: Interview with Robert W. Smith.
- KLENS-BIGMAN, D. My heart is the target: Interview with archer Shibata Kanjuro.
- LABBATE, M. Tensho kata: Goju-ryu's secret treasure.

Volume 10 • Number 2
- SVINTH, J. Karate pioneer Yabu Kentsu, 1866-1937.
- CZARNECKA, M. The saga of the modern martial arts student-instructor relationship in north American schools.
- JENSEN, M. An interview with Kwong Wing Lam on iron palm training.
- RALSTON, P. Moving beyond purely physical fighting techniques.
- TAYLOR, K. Ukemiwaza: The art of attacking in aikido.
- MALISZEWSKI, M. Don Wilson: Kickboxing champion and film star shares his perspectives.

- Berwick, S. Taiji's Chen village: Under the influence of Chen Xiaoxing.
- Berwick, S. Chen Xiaowang on learning, practicing and teaching Chen taiji.

Volume 10 • Number 3
- Kemerly, T., et al. Injuries sustained in martial arts practice.
- Mok, O. Dianxue: A genre-specific form of attack in martial arts fiction.
- Pegg, R. Chinese sword and brush masters of the Tang Dynasty (618-906).
- Goedecke, C. Isshin Kempo: Isshin-ryu's missing link to the internal.
- Yu, R. American boxing and Chinese xingyi: A comparison.
- Seidman, Y. An introduction to seizing techniques in Chen style taijiquan.
- Toth, R. An analysis of parallel techniques: The kinetic connection between Sanseru and Shishochin.
- Finch, D. Repercussions from the Douillet v.s. Shinohara's final judo bout at the 2000 Olympics in Sydney.

Volume 10 • Number 4
- Henning, S. What's in a name? The etymology of Chinese boxing.
- Florence, R. Koshin-ryu: The rebirth of Okinawa's Kojo Family martial arts.
- Profatilov, I. The traditional history of Plum Blossom Praying Mantis boxing.
- Nunberg, N. Civil and criminal liability: The martial artist's potential, part I.
- Behrendt, J. Judo and character: Moving from the hard to the gentle way.

Comments

Out of the 26 articles in Volume 10, 9 focused on China and another 9 on Japan. Only 1 on Korea. Overall, there are many styles and topics in this volume, including judo, Chen Taiji, xingyi, Plum Blossom Praying Mantis, Issin-ryu, Goju-ryu, and the Okinawan family art of Koshin-ryu. Klens-Bigman's interview with Shibata Kanjuro colors his particular style of Japanese archery. Olivia Mok presents the deadly art of pressure point striking (*dianxue*) in Chinese fictional works. Richard Pegg compares the art of the sword and Chinese calligraphy. Other topics include iron palm training, locking techniques, and martial arts training in Peking Opera.

Noah Nunberg brought an important topic for journal readers, discussing civil and criminal liability for martial artists. Another special piece as written by Russ Mason covering the fifty years of Robert W. Smith's involvement in the fighting arts. It was a nice surprise to receive an analysis by Patrick Parker on "The impact factor of the *Journal of Asian Martial Arts.*"

Of course it showed that the journal did have some positive influence after nearly ten years being published, but this was far short of what Via Media's founder had in mind.

——————— 2002 ———————

Volume 11 • Number 1
- Paz-y-Miño G., and Espinosa, A. Dichotomous keys to fundamental attacks and defenses in aikido.
- Nurchis, R. Nutrition and the role of diet in martial arts competition.
- Wingard, G. Aggressive discourse in the martial arts: An ethnographic snapshot.
- Stein, J. A comparison of Yang Style Taijiquan's large and medium frame forms.
- Nunberg, N. Civil and criminal liability: The martial artist's potential, part II.
- Labbate, M. Incorporating the main principles of kata training.

Volume 11 • Number 2
- Donohue, J. Virtual enlightenment: The martial arts, cyberspace, and American culture.
- Dohrenwend, R. The sling: Forgotten firepower of antiquity.
- Mukhopadhyay, B. War and worship: Evolution of martial music and dance in India.
- Cordes, A. Going beyond the norm: An interview with Chen Taiji stylist Wang Xian.
- Bolz, M. Kobudo: Okinawan weapons are not all flash.

Volume 11 • Number 3
- Dohrenwend, R. The odd East Asian sai.
- Svinth, J. A proper upbringing: Kendo in Canada 1900-1950.
- Allan, D. Two boys enter, two men leave: A night in Bangkok's kickboxing Thunderdome.
- Maliszewski, M. Film producer Andrè Morgan and the evolution of Asian martial arts in movies.
- Yu, R. Hong Yixiang and five fists xingyi boxing in old Taipei.
- Toth, R. Robert M. Dalgleish: 'The father of Canadian Goju-ryu karate'.

Volume 11 • Number 4
- Paz-y-Miño G., and Espinosa, A. Aikido: The art of the dynamic equiangular spiral.

- DeMarco, M. To bend or not to bend: A look at spinal movement in taijiquan and other martial arts.
- Hopkins, G. The lost secrets of Okinawan Goju-ryu: What the kata shows.
- Allan, D. Mongolian wrestling at the Nadaam 2002 Festival.
- Fu, R. Treatment of martial art injuries: East meets west.

Comments

Volume 11 includes 22 articles with 6 dealing with Japan, 4 on China, 1 on India, 1 on Southeast Asia, and 1 on Mongolia. In addition to the regular topics dealing with styles such as aikido, Chen Taiji, kendo, xingyi and Goju-ryu, some authors focused on universal subjects. Nurchis wrote about the role of diet for martial arts competition. Wingard wrote about aggressive discourse in the martial arts.

Associate Editor Robert Dohrenwend contributed two highly-detailed articles, one on the sai as found in East Asian cultures, and the ubiquitous sling. Another Associate Editor, John Donohue, utilized his background in anthropology to write "Virtual enlightenment: The martial arts, cyberspace, and American culture." Noah Nunberg followed up by providing Part II on the topic of civil and criminal liability. Mukhopadhyay, wrote on the evolution of martial music and dance in India. Allan gave readers a front seat at Bangkok's kickboxing Thunderdome.

Michael Maliszewski, another Associate Editor, stepped up with full coverage of film producer Andrè Morgan. Morgan worked on the set of Bruce Lee's *Enter the Dragon* and went on to produce many television series—including *Martial Law* and *Walker: Texas Ranger*—and movies dealing with martial arts.

―――― 2003 ――――

Volume 12 • Number 1
- Pieter, W. and Heijmans, J. Training and competition in taekwondo.
- Masciotra, D. and Monzon, M. A healthy body in a healthy mind: Striking out in time and space.
- Donohue, J. Mirror, jewel, and sword: Some thoughts on the purpose of the modern Japanese martial arts.
- Finch, D. Ulla Werbrouck: Olympic and European judo champion retires.
- Pauka, K. Silat-based Randai theater of West Sumatra makes its U.S. debut.
- Yang, T., Lianto, A. and Figler, R. Fajing: Issuing power as practiced in bajiquan and northern Chinese martial systems.
- Olson, G. Aikido, judo, and hot peppers: A true story of violence averted.

- Webster-Doyle, T. Educating the mind as well as the body through martial arts training.

Volume 12 • Number 2
- Ko, Y. Martial arts marketing: Putting the customer first.
- Wingard, G. Sport, industrialism, and the Japanese 'gentle way': Judo in late Victorian England.
- DeMarco, M. Taiwan, teachers, and training: An interview with Yang Jwingming, part I.
- Goedkoop, J. 1,000 swordmaking cuts: August events at the Kingfisher WoodWorks.
- Cruicchi, B. Larense Garrote: A Venezuelan stickfighting art.
- Donohue, D. Heiho: A tale of strategy (fiction).
- Webb, J. American judo pioneer Vince Tamura and Heiki-ryu Jujutsu.
- Dykhuizen, C.J. Sugawara Tetsutaka discusses aikido, Ueshiba Morihei, and the kagura-kotodama staff.

Volume 12 • Number 3
- Barnfield, A. Observational learning in the martial art studio: Instructors as models of positive behaviors.
- Brown, S. Dermot M. O'Neill: One of the 20th century's most overlooked combatives pioneers.
- Drape, S. How the brain learns: New teaching methodologies for the martial arts.
- Bolelli, D. Mixed martial arts: A technical analysis of the Ultimate Fighting Championship in its formative years.
- Gilbey, J. The master: Chinese boxing accounts in an envelope.
- Barnet, J. Hiroshi Ikeda's insights into aikido training.
- DeMarco, M. Taiwan, teachers, and training: An interview with Yang Jwingming, part II.

Volume 12 • Number 4
- Adrogué, M. Ancient military manuals and their relation to modern Korean martial arts.
- Berwick, S. and Butler, D. Comments on selections from Chen Xin's *Illustrated Explanations of Chen Taijiquan* with commentary from Chen Xiaowang.
- Skaggs, J. Daily life at a Muay Thai boxing camp in Phetburi.
- Toth, O. and Toth, R. Basic foundations in Okinawan karate: Interview with Canadian Tsuruoka Masami.

- FINCH, D. Okano Isao's impact on judo since the Lausanne World Championships.

Comments

Nine articles focused on Japan, 5 on China, 2 on Korea and 2 on Southeast Asia in Volume 12. These totaled 18 out of the 28 total articles in the volume. The styles ranged from Muay Thai, MMA, and taekwondo, to judo, silat, and a Venezuela stick fighting art. Other articles highlighted aspects of martial arts that can easily go unnoticed. Goedkoop's article showed what it takes to make wooden replicas of Japanese weapons. Any owner of a martial art school would be interested in Ko's pice on marketing. Since so many study a martial art in a school, Barnfield's article looks at instructors as models of positive behaviors. Drape discussed new teaching methodologies for teaching martial arts based on how the brain learns.

Many martial arts have been documented to various degrees, from simple family records to major government sponsored encyclopedias. Manuel Adrogué produced a brilliant overview in his article "Ancient military manuals and their relation to modern Korean martial arts." He presented the development of martial arts in Korean in parallel with the country's history. In addition Adrogué utilized drawings from ancient books and showed that the same postures are practiced today. Above all, he presents the martial arts as living cultural activities. This article is vital for understanding Korean martial arts and should be inspirational to others who seek to better understand martial arts in other countries by researching their historic manuels.

———— 2004 ————

Volume 13 • Number 1
- BURDICK, D., DANESHGAR, S. AND WOLSKE, J. Zurkhaneh: The Iranian house of strength.
- ZHANG, Y. AND CLARK, S. An exposition on northern China's White Ape Tongbei boxing systems.
- SODERHOLM, M. The art of conversation: Random flow training in Visayan Corto Kadena eskrima.
- HOPKINS, G. The shape of kata: The enigma of pattern.
- DEROSE, J. Again! – Practicing for perfection (fiction).

Volume 13 • Number 2
- GUTIÉRREZ, C. AND ESPARTERO, J. Jujutsu's image in Spain's wrestling shows:

A historic review.
- GAFFNEY, D. Dripping oil onto parchment: Traditional taijiquan form training in Chen village
- PAZ-Y-MIÑO, G. AND ESPINOSA, A. The rhythm of aikido, part I.
- TRAN, J. Than Quyen: An introduction to spirit forms of That Son Vietnamese martial arts.
- LOWRY, D. Kata as protection against the arbitrary.

Volume 13 • Number 3
- SEIG, B. Gravitation versus change: Explaining the relationship between personality traits and martial arts training.
- KLENS-BIGMAN, D. Chushingura: The story of the 47 masterless warriors in media.
- YANG, T., FIGLER, R., AND LIANTO, A. Basic Chinese sword training and practice.
- PAZ-Y-MIÑO, G. AND ESPINOSA, A. Music principles applied to aikido techniques, part II.
- FINCH, D. Hara-gatame: Judo's rare stomach armlock.

Volume 13 • Number 4
- HENNING, S. New light on the King Jinnaluo legend and Shaolin staff fighting.
- BARNFIELD, A. Traditional martial arts with a non-traditional population: Teaching the Deaf.
- SECOURS, K. Russian Systema flow training: A progressive alternative to stimulus-response training.
- LOUPOS, J. Taiji solo form: The benefits of group versus individual practice.
- FINCH, D. Katagaruma: Judo's spectacular shoulder wheel throw.
- TOTH, R. Yagi Meitatsu discusses the not-so-secret techniques of Okinawan Goju-ryu karate.
- DEMARCO, M. The way of brush and sword: An interview with artist Jia Lu.

Comments

Of the 22 total number of articles in Volume 13, 18 focused on martial arts originating in specific countries: 9 on Japan, 4 on China, 2 on Southeast Asia, and 1 each for Iran, Russia, and Vietnam. The specific styles in these article were White Ape Tongbei, judo, Goju-ryu, eskrima, taijiquan, aikido, jujutsu, Chinese straight sword, Vietnamese Than Quyen, Shaolin staff, Systema, and Iranian wrestling. Some articles focus on the underlying principles within the arts, such as flow training, patterns in routines, rhythm, and stimulus-response training. A major goal for the *Journal of*

Asian Martial Arts is for authors to provide detailed articles that offer information not available elsewhere, providing new details, and supported by solid references. Zhang and Clark's "An exposition on northern China's White Ape Tongbei boxing systems" is a good example of how a particular style can be covered. Gutiérrez and Espartero's scholarly approach gives a thorough coverage of the jujutsu history in Spain. Burdick and others brought a new topic to the journal with the topic of *zurkhaneh*, the traditional wrestling "houses of strength" in Iran.

Many journal articles have focused on topics that relate to teaching and learning. Ann Barnfield offers insights for teachers of traditional martial arts to deaf students. Brandon Seig's article, "Gravitation versus change: Explaining the relationship between personality traits and martial arts training," gets to the essence of why students study martial arts.

——— 2005 ———

Volume 14 • Number 1
- O'Regan, D. Jiddu Krishnamurti's influence on Bruce Lee and popular martial arts culture.
- Niiler, T. and Gong, H. The theory of lower spinal rotation: How it serves as a style-independent description of waist power.
- Bolelli, D. Varied approaches to grappling in mixed martial arts competition.
- Noble, G. Steve Arneil and the British Kyokushinkai: An interview.
- Golden, B. Using aikido principles for conflict resolution in and out of the practice hall.

Volume 14 • Number 2
- Donohue, J. Modern educational theories and traditional Japanese martial arts training methods.
- Mallon, S. Leth Wei and Khun Khmer Boran: Fighting arts of Burma and Cambodia.
- Wong, Y. From a small village to the capital: The Li Family's early taijiquan curriculum.
- Hopkins, G. The teaching of Goju-ryu kata: A brief look at methodology and practice.
- Gourley, B. Lessons in warrior strategy for both mind and eyes.
- Zerling, A. The choke: The ultimate finishing technique.

Volume 14 • Number 3
- COOPER, E. Using observational learning methods for martial arts teaching and training.
- HENNING, S. Insights from the home of xingyiquan.
- VOGEL, R. The 'ki' to a lasting marriage: The application of internal martial arts principles in the marital dojo.
- SMITH, J. (M. BILD, TRANS.) Yin style baguazhang: Hidden treasure of Chinese martial arts.
- ZERLING, A. The armlock: The technique of control.
- GRAEBNER, P. Samurai geometry: A story of values.
- JONES, L. Competition, kata and the art of judo.

Volume 14 • Number 4
- DOHRENWEND, R. The walking stick: The gentleman's weapon.
- GAFFNEY, D. Overlapping steps: Traditional training methods in Chen Village Taijiquan.
- KENNEDY, G. Yamada Yoshimitsu's influence on aikido in the west.
- CAMPBELL, P. The five katas of Yagi Meitoku.
- ZERLING, A. The leg lock: Technique of contrasts.

Comments

Volume 14 included a total of 23 articles. Twelve articles related to specific geographic areas: 6 for Japan, 5 for China, on 1 for Southeast Asia. Mallon's article covered "Leth Wei and Khun Khmer Boran: Fighting arts of Burma and Cambodia." Other authors focused on specific styles as Kyokushin karate, Goju-ryu, Li Taijiquan, Chen Taijiquan, judo, xingyiquan, baguazhang, grappling, and the combative use of a walking stick. With the help of Renzo Gracie, Andrew Zerling contributed three articles on specific techniques: the choke, armlock, and leg lock.

As an educator, Dr. Donohue contributed many articles to the journal. His article in Volume 14 Number 2, "Modern educational theories and traditional Japanese martial arts training methods," applies to all martial arts. How one thinks plays heavily on how one trains. O'Regan's article illustrates this in presenting how the philosophical teaching of Jiddu Krishnamurti influenced Bruce Lee. Individual styles can represent their fundamental philosophies, as Golden discusses in his article on utilizing aikido principles for conflict resolution. These authors are stressing a point that one's martial art practice reflects the practitioner's character.

Volume 15 • Number 1
- Looser, D. The 'risk society' and martial arts training in New Zealand.
- Zhang, Y. Shuaijiao: An introduction to the Chinese throwing art.
- Toth, R. The legacy of Dr. Richard Kim: An interview with Brian Ricci.
- Cai, N. In memory of Wu Daxin: Wu family taiji boxing gatekeeper.

Volume 15 • Number 2
- Henning, S. China's new wave of martial studies scholars.
- Suino, N. Properly gripping the sword in Muso Jikiden Eishin-ryu Iaido.
- Florence, R. Bridging traditions through eclecticism: Stephan Berwick's path to classical martial arts.
- Hobart, P. George Dillman and the influences in pressure point theory and practice.
- Finch, D. North Korean Kyu Sun Hui: An extraordinary Olympic judo player.
- Young, W. Robin. Southern Chinese lion dancing in Canada: James Lore's martial art influence.

Volume 15 • Number 3
- Donohue, J. Kaho: Cultural meaning and educational method in kata training.
- Paz-y-Miño, G., and Espinosa, A. Optical illusions in aikido.
- Saporta, J. Juan Moreno's Olympic-style training for taekwondo athletes.
- Henning, S. Che Style Xingyiquan in Taiwan as taught by Dr. Wu Chao-xiang.
- Hobart, P. Teaching nicely: Wally Jay on sharing martial principles.
- Bradley, S. Cultivating the elixir field with Sinmoo Hapkido's danjun breathing.

Volume 15 • Number 4
- Bercades, L. and Pieter, W. A biomechanical analysis of the modified taekwondo axe kick.
- Cooper, E. Information and strategies for martial arts instructors working with children diagnosed with Attention Deficit/Hyperactivity Disorder.
- Henning, S. Chinese General Yue Fei: Martial arts facts, tales, and mysteries.
- McCurry, J. and Grossman, E. The top ten errors of martial artists defending against a blade.

- TOTH, R. Masaru Shintani: The making of a modern Canadian karate master.
- HOBART, P. Integrated ideas of a life warrior: An interview with Leo Fong.

Comments

There were 22 total number of articles in Volume 15. Seven focused on China, 6 on Japan, and 3 on Korea. Styles covered in this issue included judo, iaido, Wu Taijiquan, karate, shuaijiao, xingyiquan, Hapkido, and taekwondo. A few of the specialized topics include defense against a blade, and pressure point theory and practice.

Peter Hobart contributed three articles consisting of interviews of teachers he admires and studied with over the years: Wally Jay, George Dillman, and Leo Fong. These three teachers happen to be long-time friends who have shared their knowledge between each other thus evolving their respective arts.

There are many types of students studying martial arts. Age and gender are only two factors to consider. There are more. Looser's article dives into martial arts training in New Zealand and concerns for students who may be in the "risk society." Another article, by Cooper, provides "Information and strategies for martial arts instructors working with children diagnosed with Attention Deficit/Hyperactivity Disorder." Since martial arts are part of culture, John Donohue's article looks with a broader perspective on the cultural meaning and educational method in kata training.

A major article bringing light into the state of Chinese martial arts was provided by Stanley Henning, entitled: "China's new wave of martial studies scholars." With his field research in China, personally visiting and communicating with Ma Mingda, Zhou Weiliang, and Cheng Dali. As serious martial art research is being conducted in the West, here is a reference to see what is the present state of research in China.

――――― 2007 ―――――

Volume 16 • Number 1
- DOHRENWEND, R. The spear: An effective weapon since antiquity.
- KACHUR, S., CARLETON, N., AND ASMUNDSON, G. Fear of falling: Taijiquan as a form of graded in vivo exposure therapy.
- SIMPKINS, A. AND SIMPKINS, A. Confucianism and the Asian martial traditions.
- HOBART, P. Remy Presas remembered: A perspective on life in the martial arts.
- MILLER-LANE, J. The loyal opposition and the practice of aikido.

Volume 16 • Number 2
- Pieter, W. and Heijmans, J. Development of a test for evaluating beginning taekwondo students' motor skills.
- Jeremiah, K. Asceticism and the pursuit of death by warriors and monks.
- Wolfson, G. Sanshou: Understanding taijiquan as a martial art.
- Toth, R. The stories of Meibukan Gojyu Ryu karate as told by Yagi Meitatsu.
- Webb, J. Analysis of the wing tsun punching methods.

Volume 16 • Number 3
- Khorasani, M. The magnificent beauty of edged weapons made with Persian watered steel.
- Henning, S. Ge Hong: Famous Daoist thinker and practical martial artist.
- Henning, S. The Maiden of Yue: Fount of Chinese martial arts theory.
- Hopkins, G. Politics and karate: Historical influences on the practice of Goju-ryu.
- Cheung, D. The niulang staff: A cowhearding stick as weapon.
- Kauz, H. Benefits of non-competitive push-hands practice.
- Scott, S. Core skills and four primary applications of the cross-body armlock.

Volume 16 • Number 4
- Wile, D. Taijiquan and Daoism from religion to martial art and martial art to religion.
- Câmara, F. & McKenna, M. A preliminary analysis of Goju-ryu kata structure.
- Chaudhuri, J. Wing chun's chum kiu form: A study in stability and mobility.
- Rymaruk, I. Defending to the four directions: Evolving Uechi-ryu's hojoun-do exercises for advanced students.

Comments
Volume 16 included a total of 21 articles with 16 on specific geographic areas: China with 9, Japan with 5, and Korea and the Philippines each with 1. Some styles covered were Goju-ryu, Uechi-ryu, taijiquan, taekwondo, and aikido. There were some special presentations dealing with weapons, including the Chinese cowhearding staff. Associate Editor Robert Dohrenwend dove deep into his library to produce "The spear: An effective weapon since antiquity." Khorasani's well-written and illustrated article broke new ground for the journal, presenting "The magnificent beauty of edged weapons made with Persian watered steel." Peter Hobart added an article on Remy Presas and Modern Arnis, completing a four-part series

started in the previous volume.

As in the Chinese concept of a balance between *wen* and *wu* (scholar/warrior), this volume had a good balance with the cultural aspect. The Simpkins contributed "Confucianism and the Asian martial traditions." Douglas Wile provided an extensive piece on "Taijiquan and Daoism from religion to martial art and martial art to religion." Ken Jeremiah focused on the ascetic aspects of monks and warriors. In two articles, Stanley Henning introduced many to the thought of Ge Hong and the story of the Maiden of Yue—both having had an impact on martial traditions.

A blessing of studying martial arts can be discovering how the theory and practice may offer insights for improving other aspects in our lives. From the title "The loyal opposition and the practice of aikido," you could guess that Jonathan Miller-Lane's article would show how important it is to have realistic attacks in order to foster practical defensive skills. He does this well. In addition, he brings in an old British concept of "loyal opposition" from 1826 a phrase that came to denote a political party or group of parties. The nearly 200 year-old concept is helpful to understand martial arts and opposing viewpoints.

―――― 2008 ――――

Volume 17 • Number 1
- COHEN, K. Taiji ruler: Legacy of the sleeping immortal.
- EBELL, B. Competition versus tradition in Kodokan judo.
- LANG, T. Conveying combative movement in print: How to present techniques in photographs and text.
- KHORASANI, M. Reviving the ancient art of making Persian crucible steel for bladed weaponry.
- GATLING, L. The First Kodokan Judo Kata International Competition and its katas.
- LAJCIK, T. Developing fighting technique through visualization.

Volume 17 • Number 2
- CYNARSKI, W. An overview of Polish martial arts.
- SCOTT, S. The Kharbarelli pick-up: How and why this throwing technique works.
- LAM, W. AND ALAMUDEEN, S. The dynamic impact of the tiger within Chinese martial arts.
- BIALOKUR, N. AND VLAD, I. Asian martial art exhibitions at the Swiss Castle of Morges.

- GAFFNEY, D. Chenjiagou: The history of the taiji village.

Volume 17 • Number 3
- PATTERSON, W. Bushido's role in the growth of pre-World War II Japanese nationalism.
- MASON, R. Zheng Manqing: The memorial hall and legacy of the master of five excellences in Taiwan.
- KOEPFER, S. Offensive rolling in sambo.
- WADA, S. Kendo and shodo in life: A long-lasting association between the way of the sword and the brush.
- HOBART, P. AND WOLFE, R. The parry: An essential free-fighting tool.

Volume 17 • Number 4
- KO, Y. AND YANG, J. The globalization of martial arts: The change of rules for new markets.
- NEIDE, J. Japan's future: Embracing multi-ethnic complexities through physical education and the martial arts.
- HENNING, S. Visiting Tianshui city: A look into martial culture on China's northern Silk Route
- SECOURS, K. Takedown defenses of Russian Systema.
- BURROUGHS, J. A comprehensive introduction to Sun Family Taiji boxing: Theory and applications.
- MURAKAMI, K. (Q. OGA-BALDWIN, TRANS.) Renkoho: Maintaining a flexible body for health and longevity.

Comments

There are 22 articles in Volume 17. Fourteen articles are associated with these geographic areas: China and Japan each with 6, and Russia with 2. The main styles discussed are judo, kendo, Chen Taijiquan, Yang Taijiquan, Sun Taijiquan, Russian Systema and Sambo. Other articles looked at individual techniques as the Kharbarelli pick-up, parry, and the use of visualizing techniques to improve skill level. Wing Lam and Alamudeen's article focused on the tiger symbol and applications.

Bialokur and Vlad contributed an excellent report on "Asian martial art exhibitions at the Swiss Castle of Morges" which included many styles of martial arts and teachers from a number of European countries. This is almost in contrast to Neide's article on "Japan's future: Embracing multi-ethnic complexities through physical education and the martial arts," since the Japanese are more recently adapting to the inclusion of students of other ethnicities.

A major influencer in Europe noted for his research as well as organizing academic conferences and publications mainly on Asian martial arts, Dr. Wojciech Cynarski, offered our journal readers an excellent overview of Polish martial arts. His lengthy scholarly work includes the background of Polish history, a review of related literature, museum illustrations of weaponry (famous for their spears and swords) and battles, and modern schools that have preserved the rich traditions. Such a wonderful work is insightful for learning about Polish martial traditions, but also proves most useful in comparison with Asian traditions.

——— 2009 ———

Volume 18 • Number 1
- WINGARD, G. Building men on the mat: Traditional manly arts and the Asian martial arts in America.
- BERWICK, S., ET AL. Qingping straight sword: The last remaining Chinese sword system?
- TAYLOR, K. Progressive instruction inherent in standardized form practice using iaido for illustration.
- SHERIDAN, B. From the tatami mat to the printed page: Author Barry Eisler keeps his fiction real.
- ANTA, J. Shaolin physical conditioning: What's old is new again.

Volume 18 • Number 2
- HLINAK, M. Judo comes to California: Judo vs. wrestling in the American West, 1900-1920.
- OVERILL, R. Was Jesus a martial artist?
- HOBART, P. Of packs and lone wolves: Interview with Ellis Amdur regarding Japanese martial traditions.
- WEBB, J. Tactile reflex development through wing tsun's 'sticking hands' practice.
- PITTMAN, A. A universal martial tactic: The shoulder throw and its variations.

Volume 18 • Number 3
- KELLAND, M. Psychology, physical disability and the application of Buddhist mindfulness to martial arts programs.
- DEMARCO, M. Xiong Style Taiji in Taiwan: Historical development and a photographic exposé featuring Master Lin Jianhong.
- MACARAEG, R. Pirates of the Philippines: A critical thinking exercise.

- ROWE, M., AND WEDLAKE, L. The carotid choke: To sleep, perchance to die?
- BAILEY, T. Arthur Rosenfeld: Martial artist and storyteller.

Volume 18 • Number 4
- HACKNEY, C. The Aristotelian philosophy of the martial arts.
- JONES, B. Skin infections in the grappling arts.
- HOPKINS, G. Kata and bunkai: A study in theme and variations in karate's solo practice routines.
- CARTMELL, T. Throwing techniques in the internal martial arts: An elucidation of the guiding principle of 'sticking and following'.
- BRYANT, A. Eishin-ryu's poetic tradition for transmitting secrets of swordmanship.

Comments

Volume 18 seems to include an even broader range of topics than previous issues. There are 20 articles total with 11 specific to a geographic area: 5 each for China and Japan and 1 for the Philippines. Styles focused on include karate, Eishin-ryu, wing tsun, Shaolin, iaido, and the Qingping straight sword. Some authors wrote about specific techniques, these being the shoulder throw and the carotid choke, and — on wider scale — kata applications and throwing techniques from the Chinese arts of taiji, xingyi, and bagua.

Two articles stem from studies in Asia. Peter Hobart contributed "Of packs and lone wolves: Interview with Ellis Amdur regarding Japanese martial traditions." Amdur has long been respected for his first-hand experience and skills derived from his studies in Japan. My own piece results from studies of a particular taijiquan style in Taiwan: "Xiong Style Taiji in Taiwan: Historical development and a photographic exposé featuring Master Lin Jianhong.

In this particular volume, articles were strong on martial arts and character. Wingard's article is titled "Building men on the mat: Traditional manly arts and the Asian martial arts in America." An excellent tie-in is the piece by Hlinak's "Judo comes to California: Judo vs. wrestling in the American West, 1900-1920." And we find a balance between Eastern and Western school of thought: Kelland's application of Buddhist mindfulness to martial arts programs, and Hackney's "The Aristotelian philosophy of the martial arts."

Volume 19 • Number 1
- DOHRENWEND, R. Dangerous animals and the Asian martial arts.
- FILIPIAK, K. From warrior to sportsmen: How traditional Chinese martial arts adapted to modernity.
- SYMMES, E. Is there a warrior within?
- GAUTHIER, M. Aikido as myth.
- NEIDE, J. Forty years of martial art training and almost sixty years old.
- PITTMAN, A. Training the lower body for better stances, steps, and kicks.
- BURROUGHS, J. North star: Head butting as a weapon in Chinese martial arts.

Volume 19 • Number 2
- VEY, G. Integrative combat: An empirical perspective of the martial arts.
- BRADLEY, S. The pineal gland's biochemical function in the fighting and meditative arts exemplified in Korean Sinmoo Hapkido.
- SMITH, P., NIILER, T., AND McCULLOUGH, P. Evaluating makiwara punching board performance.
- LO, B., ET AL. Liu Xiheng: Memories of a taiji sage (Compiled and edited by Russ Mason).
- ROMÀN, F. AND GUTIÉRREZ, C. Comprehensive penitentiary defense as developed for use in Spain.

Volume 19 • Number 3
- PIETER, W. Talent detection in taekwondo practitioners.
- ACEVEDO, W. AND CHEUNG, M. A historical overview of mixed martial arts in China.
- SCHNEIDER, S. Learning India's martial art of kalarippayattu: Unsettled ecologies of gender, class culture, and ethnicity.
- KLENS-BIGMAN, D. Fighting women of Kabuki theater and the legacy of women's Japanese martial arts.
- GRAYCAR, M. AND TOMLINSON, R. Tensegrity: Development of dynamic balance and internal power in taijiquan.
- DEMARCO, M. Practical fighting strategies of Indonesian kuntao-silat in the Willem Reeders tradition.

Volume 19 • Number 4
- JONES, L., AND HANON, M. The way of kata in Kodokan Judo.
- PITTMAN, A. Conditioning the axis of the body: Martial and yogic training

methods, east and west.
- SUENAKA, R. AND TAYLOR, C. Aikido defenses against real-world attacks.
- JOERN, T. How baguazhang incorporates theory from the *Book of Changes.*

Comments

Volume 19 has 22 total number of articles with 15 focusing on specific countries: 6 for China, 5 for Japan, 2 for Korea, and 1 each for India and Indonesia. Authors who have written on a specific style, covered judo kata, aikido, baguazhang, taijiquan, kuntao-silat, kalarippayattu, taekwondo, Sinmoo Hapkido, and makiwara training.

Keeping physically fit is one of the goals for martial art practitioners. Allan Pittman contributed two extraordinary articles in this area: (1) "Training the lower body for better stances, steps, and kicks," and (2) "Conditioning the axis of the body: Martial and yogic training methods, east and west."

Sinologist Kai Filipiak offers a clear perspective on the evolution of Chinese martial arts in his scholarly article "From warrior to sportsmen: How traditional Chinese martial arts adapted to modernity." There is certainly a drive to bring Chinese martial arts into the sporting area, as taekwondo highlights what is possible, including being an Olympic sport. This is Dr. Willy Pieter area of specialization. He wrote "Talent detection in taekwondo practitioners."

Since ancient times, martial arts developed in large part as defense against animals. Much credit to Associate Editor Robert Dohrenwend for his insightful academic work in producing "Dangerous animals and the Asian martial arts." For any martial artist who has a chance of crossing paths with a dangerous animal, as while hunting or hiking in the mountains, this article could be a lifesaver.

———— 2011 ————

Volume 20 • Number 1
- MOENIG, U. The evolution of kicking techniques in taekwondo.
- MACARAEG, R. Sorting out categories of bladed weaponry using the Persian revival sword as an example.
- EDINBOROUGH, C. Self-reflection and the organization of experience: Examining Inaba Minoru's budo as a form of art.
- YANG, N. Reflecting on traditional martial arts: Past, present, and future.
- LABBATE, M. Attention, sit, meditate, bow, ready position: Ritualized dojo pattern or character training?

- MOSHER, H. Form and function: Why push-hands is essential to the practice of taijiquan.

Volume 20 • Number 2
- BROWN, S. Multiple intelligences in the process of learning martial arts using taijiquan as an example.
- WELLS, M. AND HENNING, S. Boxer Zhang Songxi and the origins of the internal-external school concept.
- LINDEN, P. Aikido and body-awareness training for peacemaking and combat.
- WEBB, J. A study in maximizing speed through ving tsun concepts.
- ROXBOROUGH, S. Capoeira: Brazil's martial and cultural art form.
- FERGUSON, R. A study of armbar submissions in Ultimate Fighting Championship contests from 2000 to 2011.
- MCKENNA, M. Nahate: The old school Okinawan martial art and its original four-kata curriculum, part I.
- PEGG, R. Ancient Chinese bronze swords in the MacLean Collection.

Volume 20 • Number 3
- DALIA, A. Fighting heros: The core values of the xia tradition in early China.
- DAVISON, P. Issues concerning board breaking.
- LOONG, L.H. Cultural myths: Unpacking the origins of Muay Thai.
- MCKENNA, M. Nahate: The old school Okinawan martial art and its original four-kata curriculum, part II.
- BAEK, B. Three techniques of dantian rotation in Chen Taiji internal energy techniques and their relationship with the body's meridians.
- DICRISTOFANO, A. Oshigata: Appreciating Japanese sword tracings for their reference and beauty.
- YIANNAKIS, L. A taxonomy of principles used in judo throwing techniques.

Volume 20 • Number 4
- VAN RHEENEN, D. Reflections on an after-school literacy program and the educational value of taekwondo: A preliminary analysis.
- FERGUSON, R. A study of chokehold submissions in Ultimate Fighting Championships from 2000 to 2011.
- PAUL, J. Teaching aikido to children with Autism Spectrum Disorders.
- SHEETZ-RUNKLE, B. Why women need Sunzi's *Book on the Art of War*.
- ZHENG S. Wushu's transformation from the local boxing ring to the world stage: Globalization's impact and implications on the evolution of Chinese martial arts.

Comments

There is a total of 26 articles in Volume 20. Twenty of these are associated with these geographic areas: China and Japan with 8 each, Korea with 2, and 1 each for Brazil and Thailand. Articles focused on aikido, wushu, MMA, taekwondo, Capoeira, judo, Chen Taijiquan, karate, Muay Thai, and Ving Tsun. One of the topics here, by DiCristofano, focused on the beauty of *oshigata*—the aesthetic, highly-detailed tracing of Japanese blades. Davison wrote "Issues concerning board breaking," and Dalia wrote of the *xia*, the topic of martial heros in this specialized genre.

In two separate articles, Ferguson presented his research findings on two of the most common techniques used in MMA, the armbar and the chokehold utilized in the Ultimate Fighting Championships from 2000 to 2011. In his article "The evolution of kicking techniques in taekwondo," Moening analyzes early karate and taekwondo literature, including diverse and varied Korean sources. Dr. Richard Pegg, a scholar of Asian studies and art curator with over thirty years of studies in the martial arts, writes on ancient Chinese bronze swords.

———— 2012-2016 ————

Volume 21 • Number 1
- RHOADS, C.J., CRIDER, D., AND HAYDUK, D. Taiji and qigong health benefits: How and why they work.
- PIETER, W. Physique, body fat, and martial arts performance correlations found in adult elite karate and taekwondo athletes.
- ROMÀN, F. Using gradual force and applying techniques: From the system of Comprehensive Penitentiary Defense.
- THARP, A. Nihonto: A legal perspective on Japanese swords and their intrinsic value.
- HOBART, P. Changes in the martial artist's right to bear arms.
- BRODSKY, G. Yoga alchemy in taijiquan.
- ZERLING, A. Sumo wrestling: Practical techniques for the martial arts.

Volume 22 • Number 1
- WARD, P. Sword-cutting practice of feudal Japan: Anatomical considerations of tameshigiri.

Volume 23 • Number 1
- WINBORNE, D. An exploration of the Bando system and other ancient Burmese fighting traditions: History and current practices.

- YIANNAKIS, L. Rhythm, patterns, and timing in martial arts as exemplified through judo.

2016 Volume 25 • Number 1
- JONES, L., SAVAGE, M., AND GATLING, L. Kodokan judo's self-defense system—Kodokan Goshin-jutsu.

Comments

Volume 21 Number 1 was the final full issue of the *Journal of Asian Martial Arts*. In order to accomodate authors, we decided to publish a few more important articles in the following years, producing Volumes 22, 23, and 25. There were 11 total articles published with 8 focusing on arts associated with specific geographic locations: 4 for Japan, 2 for China, 1 each for Korea and Myanmar (Burma). The authors' subjects included taiji/qigong, Bando, judo, karate, taekwondo, sumo, and Japanese swords.

Romàn contributed a follow-up piece on the system of Comprehensive Penitentiary Defense, a very practical system for using gradual force and applying techniques in prisons. With his academic specialization on martial sports, Associate Editor Willy Pieter offers a perspective on "Physique, body fat, and martial arts performance correlations found in adult elite karate and taekwondo athletes."

The last two articles published deal with aspects of judo of great interest to serious practitioners. One by Linda Yiannakis is titled "Rhythm, patterns, and timing in martial arts as exemplified through judo." The other article is by Llyr Jones, Martin Savage, and Lance Gatling, titled "Kodokan judo's self-defense system: Kodokan Goshin-jutsu."

As the journal was nearing an end, I was invited by the Faculty of Sports Studies at Masaryk University in the Czech Republic to lecture for a week in November 2015. They have a wonderful program with a strong focus on martial traditions. I spoke on topics of martial arts research and academic publishing and taught a practical taijiquan class.

Chapter V

Other Via Media Publications

Anthologies
By ceasing publication of the *Journal of Asian Martial Arts* came the prospect that the articles would no longer be available. The quality and content of each article make them valuable references. One way to keep the articles available was to publish them in anthologies in both print and ebook formats, organized by a common theme. Anyone interested in a particular geographic area or style could find appropriate anthologies. Fifty-five anthologies were published listed below by year of publication.

- (2015). *Cheng Man-ch'ing and t'ai chi: Echoes in the hall of happiness.*
- (2015). *Chen T'ai Chi: Traditional instructions from the Chen Village, vol. 1.*
- (2015). *Chen T'ai Chi: Traditional instructions from the Chen Village, vol. 2.*
- (2015). *America's fascination with Asian martial arts.*
- (2015). *Chinese swords: An ancient tradition and modern training.*
- (2015). *Dohrenwend's masterwork: On the spear, sling, sai, and walking stick.*
- (2015). *Indo-Malay martial traditions: Aesthetics, mysticism, and combatives, vol. 1.*
- (2015). *Indo-Malay martial traditions: Aesthetics, mysticism, and combatives, vol. 2.*
- (2015). *Intrinsic values of the Japanese sword.*
- (2015). *Judo and American culture—Prelude, acceptance, embodiment.*
- (2015). *Karate kata: For the transmission of high-level combative skills, vol. 1.*
- (2015). *Karate kata: For the transmission of high-level combative skills, vol. 2.*
- (2015). *Medieval warrior cultures of Europe and Japan: Body, mind, sword.*
- (2015). *Mixed martial arts: Analyses of techniques and usage.*
- (2015). *T'ai chi and qigong for your health: Historical and scientific foundations.*
- (2015). *Taekwondo studies: Advanced theory and practice.*
- (2016). *Aikido: O-sensei's sublime synthesis, vol. 1.*

- (2016). *Aikido: O-sensei's sublime synthesis, vol. 2.*
- (2016). *Asian martial arts in literature and movies.*
- (2016). *Bagua and xingyi: An intersection of the straight and curved.*
- (2016). *Draeger: Pioneering leader in Asian martial traditions.*
- (2016). *Judo kata: Practice, competition, purpose.*
- (2016). *Lesser-known tai chi lineages: Li, Wu, Sun, Xiong.*
- (2016). *Mantis Boxing anthology.*
- (2016). *The martial arts business arena: Investment, politics, profit.*
- (2016). *Realistic martial arts for violence and peace: Law, enforcement, defense.*
- (2016). *Sambo and Systema: Russia's prominent martial arts.*
- (2016). *Taekyon: The Korean martial art.*
- (2016). *Wing Chun: Writings for advanced practitioners.*
- (2016). *Women and Asian martial traditions.*
- (2016). *Okinawan martial traditions: Te, tode, karate, karatedo, kobudo, vol. 1.*
- (2016). *Okinawan martial traditions: Te, tode, karate, karatedo, kobudo, vol. 2.*
- (2017). *Okinawan martial traditions: Te, tode, karate, karatedo, kobudo, vol. 3.*
- (2017). *Academic approaches to martial arts research.*
- (2017). *Filipino martial art anthology.*
- (2017). *Foundations of Korean martial arts: Masters, manuals and combative techniques.*
- (2017). *Southeast Asian martial arts: Cambodia, Myanmar, Thailand, Vietnam.*
- (2017). *The sword in Japanese martial traditions.*
- (2017). *Tai chi odyssey: History and practice methods.*
- (2017). *Tai chi and the Daoist spirit.*
- (2017). *Teaching and learning Japanese martial arts: Scholarly perspectives, vol. 1.*
- (2017). *Teaching and learning Japanese martial arts: Scholarly perspectives, vol. 2.*
- (2018). *Conditioning for martial art practice: Nutrition, exercise, energy, strength, flexibility.*
- (2018). *Henning's scholarly works on Chinese combative traditions.*
- (2018). *Jujutsu and judo in the west.*
- (2018). *Martial arts in the arts: An appreciation of artifacts.*
- (2019). *Grappling and throwing from the near and far east.*
- (2020). *An anthology of Chinese martial arts.*

- (2020). *Asian martial arts, monks, and ways of thought.*
- (2020). *Chinese combatives: An anthology.*
- (2020). *Chinese martial arts: Changing views and practices.*
- (2020). *Japanese weapons: An anthology.*
- (2020). *Martial and healing traditions of India.*
- (2020). *Martial arts instruction for children—Special concerns for teachers and parents.*
- (2020). *Some western pioneers in Asian martial arts.*

Books

Via Media was fortunate to work with two of the leading martial art writers of the mid-twentieth century. The first was Robert w. Smith. Known as a world's leading authority on Asian martial arts, Smith practiced, taught, and wrote on the Asian martial arts for more than fifty years. From his late teens he trained under eminent Western boxing and wrestling coaches and later immersed himself in judo and finally the Chinese martial arts under celebrated masters. He taught many students in the latter arts in the Washington D.C. area where he worked as an intelligence officer for the CIA.

Smith enjoyed the journal and contributed ten articles. When he asked about publishing his 400-page memoir, I was thrilled. *Martial Musings: A Portrayal of Martial Arts in the 20th Century (1999)* was Smith fourteenth and final book—a broad, somewhat historical, semi-autobiographical commentary on martial arts in the 20th century.

Just after publishing *Martial Musings*, Oscar Ratti and Adele Westbrook began to discuss the possibility of Via Media Publishing a three-volume graphic novel series. They had a distinguished reputation as the authors of two books that have long been recognized as classic publications: *Secrets of the Samurai*, and *Aikido and the Dynamic Sphere*. Their trilogy published by Via Media was *Tales of the Hermit*, a captivating, inspirational story of a Western pilgrim who journeyed to Japan in the 1600s. Oscar had a special talent for illustrating combative figures. His artwork appeared many times in the journal and was featured on covers as well.

The books mentioned above were produced while the journal was still being published. After the last journal was published, I decided to produce a book that would include writings by some of the writers who had articles in the journal. It was titled *Asian Martial Arts: Constructive Thoughts and Practical Application* (2012). This book represents an international gathering of friends who happen to be highly qualified martial art scholars and practitioners. We came together in celebration of the more than twenty years the *Journal of Asian Martial Arts* inspired scholarship in this field to higher academic standards while encouraging all aspects of responsible practice. The book was not in the academic style for which the journal was noted. It was produced in a spirit of joy.

After the journal ceased being produced, I thought it was too difficult to continue publishing. However, a number of authors sought out Via Media for publishing their works. I couldn't say no to Jan Kauskas manuscript submission. I loved his fictional work, *Laoshi: Tai Chi, Teachers, and Pursuit of Principle* (2014). In the story, a taiji student explores the Dao of Zheng Manqing (Cheng Man-ch'ing) with the aid of his teacher, Laoshi. Kauskas' follow-up work is about the student-turned-teacher: *Laoshi's legacy: Emergence from shadow* (2018).

In 2015 a former neighbor in Erie, PA, Gino Carlotti, asked if I'd help him publish a collection of personal accounts of growing up in an Italian-American home in an inter-city neighborhood of the 1930s, 40s, and 50s. Accompanying the text are 52 pictures of an historical era many Americans hold close to their hearts and consider the most precious of their lives. The book fondly enlivens themes of America's melting pot. The title is *Flashbacks From the Other Side of the Tracks*.

In 2019 another friend and leading exponent of Arthur Sykes' kuntao system, Reginald McKissick, submitted a manuscript. Information for the book came from him along with his student Dexter Parker and edited by Alejandro Rooney. The result was *The Liu Seong Kuntao Broken Mirror System*. McKissick followed Sykes closely for decades. The book is a rare reference for this branch of Willem Reeders kuntao.

In the following year, 2020, Via Media published *Mundunur: A Mountain Village Under the Spell of South Italy*. Not a martial art topic! But there is some tie-in. One of my best friends, Richard Lopez, had passed away in June 2014. Less than a year before that, in April 2013, Thomas Pepperman passed. These two were life-long friends and kuntao mentors. Along with these losses, my parents, sister, aunt and uncle had also passed within a six year period. Without family around, I decided to go to Italy to feel some family roots. My grandparents were born in a village called Montenero Val Cocchiara, in Molise province, just east of Rome. In the local dialect it is called Mundunur. Lopez's mother was also from this small village. While there, I taught taijiquan at a local resort.

When I returned from the Italy trip in 2014, a relative said I should write a book about the village. I took on the task. I returned to Italy in 2017 to conduct research. The same year I revisited Taiwan. I actually felt a closer kinship in Taiwan among my "taiji family" than with blood relatives in Italy. The research and writing of the Italy book took five years of full-time work. In 2020 I published it in English. In 2020 the book was translated into Italian and published by Gruppo Albatros in Rome as *Mundunur: Un paese di montagna sotto l'incantesimo del sud Italia*. I later published an Italian language version under Via Media (2022).

The fastidious writing necessary for the Italy book, especially under pressure to complete it as early as possible, was very laborious. After this big project I searched for another project that would be more fun to do. Thus came the idea of a fictional story about martial arts. The book's title is *Martial Art Essays from Beijing, 1760,* published in 2021. The themes in this book—drawn from Chinese history, culture, and martial arts experience—are entwined in a fictional narrative to animate events envisaged to have occurred during the mid-eighteenth century. A thin veil separates fact from fiction. It was translated into Chinese and published in 2022 as 武术随笔北京1760年.

When compared with the academic journal articles, anthologies, and the book on Italy, the fictional *Martial Art Essays* book was pure pleasure to produce. A very different category of writing, with more creativity and freedom for the imagination. At the same time, the content in a fictional book can be as important as any scholarly tome.

My next work included some martial themes, but should be of interest to anyone who likes crime and mystery novels. The title is *Wuxia America: The Emergence of a Chinese American Hero* (2023). Chinese martial artists may know that *wuxia* means "martial hero." The plot is spiced like a Chinese herbal recipe. The main character is a Chinese American doctor, Dr. Lou, who becomes the target of an international criminal ring.

The most recent publication is *Reflections on Mainland China and Taiwan* (2023), compiled by Michael Stone. This is a multi-disciplinary collection of research articles on East Asia by twelve scholars from my alma mater Seton Hall University's Asian Studies program. It encompasses a broad range of topics covering philosophy and religion, history, international relations, language, and culture. It includes a history of Seton Hall's Chinese program, one of the earliest such curricula in the United States.

Outside of the 81 *Journal of Asian Martial Arts* issues and 55 resulting anthologies, we have the additional 15 book titles discussed above. You can see that the book projects started with authors who were involved with the journal. Other books came about because of longtime friendships established since childhood or from university days. For decades I've helped others to publish their valuable works. But, the biggest change since bringing the journal and anthology work to a close has been a personal focus on my own writings.

What is next? Ideas are percolating. Perhaps some will inspire me to write more books, plant a garden, or bake some bread. I'll certainly keep practicing and teaching martial arts.

Books Published by Via Media

- SMITH, R. (1999). *Martial musings: A portrayal of martial arts in the 20th century.*
- RATTI, O. AND WESTBROOK, A. (2001). *Tales of the hermit, vol. I: The castle in the rain and the judge.*
- RATTI, O. AND WESTBROOK, A. (2001). *Tales of the hermit, vol. II: Yamabushi and homecoming.*
- RATTI, O. AND WESTBROOK, A. (2004). *Tales of the hermit, vol. II: The monk and the samurai, the sword maiden, and the katana that caused it all.*
- DEMARCO, M., ET AL. (2012). *Asian martial arts: Constructive thoughts and practical application.*
- KAUSKAS, J. (2014). *Laoshi: Tai chi, teachers, and pursuit of principle.*
- CARLOTTI, G. (2015). *Flashbacks from the other side of the tracks.*
- KAUSKAS, J. (2018). *Laoshi's legacy: Emergence from shadow.*
- MCKISSICK, R., PARKER, D., AND ROONEY, A. (2019). *The Liu Seong kuntao broken mirror system.*
- DeMarco, M. (2020). *Mundunur: A mountain village under the spell of south Italy.*
- DEMARCO, M. (2021). *Martial art essays from Beijing, 1760.*
- DEMARCO, M. (2022) 武术随笔北京1760年 (Martial art essays from Beijing, 1760).
- DI MARCO, M. (DEMARCO, M.) (2022). *Mundunur: Un paese di montagna sotto l'incantesimo del sud Italia* (Mundunur: A mountain village under the spell of south Italy).
- STONE, M., ET AL. (2023). *Reflections on mainland China and Taiwan.*
- DEMARCO, M. (2023). *Wuxia America: The emergence of a Chinese American hero.*

Chapter VI

Transferring a Martial Tradition

After ten years of kuntao studies, I had the opportunity to go to Taiwan to study taijiquan. My first time there was in 1976, mainly learning the traditional long routine. Getting ready to return to the US, my teacher told me not to teach. I didn't. During the following years, I returned to Taiwan a few more times to continue studies. After seventeen years studying taiji, I began teaching in 1992, about the same time I founded Via Media Publishing. This is a total of twenty-seven years in the martial arts before starting to teach. Perhaps I should have waited another ten years before teaching?

In the Far East, there is a strong tradition of respect for the elderly. With more years comes more experience, knowledge, and skills. This is highly applicable in martial art instruction. We see it in traditional titles for teachers, such as the Chinese *laoshi* and Japanese *sensei*, both titles embedding the meaning of an elder who possesses years of experience.

Teaching and Learning in Erie, PA

My hometown, Erie, PA, is where I started teaching taijiquan. Meeting twice a week, classes were mainly held at the second-floor studio of friend and mentor, Richard "Dick" Lopez, at 1012 West 27th Street. Dick would often be at the studio, keeping an eye on my classes and adding his humor to the atmosphere. Sometimes he'd be inspired and share some practical insights into a technique or tell a story from his past martial studies.

Lopez provided a nice space, mainly built by his own hands with the help of a few of his dedicated students. From the entrance door was a narrow room with a desk and a long bench. This area had much memorabilia, including photographs of Willem Reeders behind the desk, broadsword, taichus, a Buddha statue, and a CD player. Dick could often be found at the desk, filing taichus or knife blades while listening to some jazz. In the desk were stacks or printed documents and other martial art-related items. A very small dressing room was behind the desk area, separated by a wall. Workout clothing hung on a wall, and others weapons Dick made where stored inside an enclosed bench.

After class: Amy Eisenberg, Judith Johnston, the author, and George Berardini.

In the main room a 4x8 foot painted dragon hung on one wall. Another wall was covered with mirrors, which made the room feel much larger. A couple pulleys were screwed into a ceiling rafter for hoisting heavy punching bags. Wrestling mats were stacked against one wall for whenever needed. On the wall next to the dragon were a set of taichu and two taiji straight swords.

Besides having such a nice workout area, a blessing was Dick's presence and support. I had some longtime students over the years at his studio, the most memorable being George Bernardini, Judith Johnston, Bill Steff, Amy Eisenberg, Betty Thumma, Sr. Patricia "Sister Knuckles" Whalen, and Richard Stubenhoffer. During the nice summer months we held classes on the peaceful campus of Villa Maria Academy at 2403 West 8th Street. We practiced behind a school building in very large area with manicured lawn and some trees. Classes met twice a week for an hour and a half, but here we'd often stay longer, enjoying the outdoors.

Student stories are worth noting, if nothing but for the entertainment and perhaps for insight into taiji principles. First to come to mind stems from working on applications with Betty Thumma. I was standing in front of her and she grabbed my right wrist with great strength with her right hand. While stepping around her right side, my right hand circled down and then up behind her back. She was in agony by the torque in her arm. Behind her, I whispered in her ear: "Betty, let go." I was not holding onto her. She was holding onto my wrist and wouldn't let go. For taiji, we constantly look for ways not to be tense, but often we just bring it on ourselves.

On another occasion students were talking about international travel and feeling confident that, if there came a need, they would be able to use their taiji for self-defense. As soon as I heard this, I had them sit on one side of the room, then asked each student to come on the floor one by one.

I would attack, without any set-up. The student would not know the angle of attack or what technique would be used, a punch, push, kick, or grab... From twenty feet away, I quickly ran toward Judith Johnston. She put up her arms in front to cover her face and leaned back from the onslaught. Inches away, I slowed and simply placed my index fingers on her shoulder blades with slight pressure. Because she was tense and leaning backwards, the light touch was enough to set her in motion. As her top half lead, her legs couldn't keep up. Her arms started to flap in an effort to regain balance. The fluttering was futile. With body angled, she kept floating backward, somewhat like a swimmer doing backstrokes, until her back hit the wall. Two straight swords displayed on the wall fell at her sides. — Just because we've studied some self-defense techniques doesn't mean they will work on the street. That takes another level of practice which is more realistic than set-up applications at relatively slow speed.

In some martial art traditions, such as Reeders kuntao, a top student is often called the Golden Boy. If I had one, it would be George Berardini. He's the only student who trained to a level where he could use his taiji for real combat. He studied Yang and Chen styles with me and some kuntao. George has a million entertaining tales, but we'll give one example.

George worked as Chief of the Electical Department for the City of Erie. One day he was walking down the main street to go into the municipal building. A lady was walking toward George, noticed him, and made a movement to guard her purse. George notice this as well as a man walking behind her who started to pass her on her right side. He grabbed the purse! Just steps away, George dashed forward in a "brush knee push posture," striking the man's right shoulder. As George did this, his arm went through the purse loops and the purse fell onto George's elbow near his bicept. The man was stunned, saying it was his purse. George replied with a grin: "Try to take it." The man ran off and the purse was returned to the lady.

It is a blessing when taiji can be used with good results. George had proper training. Others were more typical taiji players focused on it for health. Usually taiji students are older too. I miss the old kuntao days when we worked hard on applications and sparred. The past training stays with you, but the combative elements rarely come into taiji classes at the realistic level. I was surprised when a professional boxer asked me to help her train in private classes for nine months. It was a way for me to see how I can move after so many years away from sparring. It proved very easy because she was trained in a hard boxing method and the relaxed taiji principles worked for me with ability to move in and out according to the encounters. It was fun!

I came up with the name Winged Lion School of Tai Chi as a metaphor of the taiji principles of lightness and strength. There is a bronze of a winged lion in The British Museum that dates from the Sung Dynasty (960–1279). There are wings on both sides of the lion. The body itself is inlaid with silver and gold with stylized birds. George Bernardini ordered a print of it for our school. It hung on the wall at the Lopez studio for years. It was reproduced on the back of our school shirts.

Outside of my own classes, I taught for short periods at the Hamot Hospital Wellness Center on 300 State Street and also at the LECOM Medical Fitness and Wellness Center on 5401 Peach Street. I prefered my own classes where everyone got to know each other well.

Teaching and Learning in Santa Fe, NM

I moved to Santa Fe, New Mexico, the "Land of Enchantment", in 2004. Before moving, I had sent a resume to Santa Fe Community College to see if they could use a taiji teacher in their physical education department. They said sorry, but a teacher was already well established at the institute. It would have helped me settle, knowing I would have some steady income. The week I arrived and found an apartment, I received an email from the college. The taiji teacher had quit and I could start the following Monday.

In addition to classes at the community college, I found rental space for my own taiji classes. With some promotion, students arrived. Over the years, I rented at other locations, primarily for the winter months, including the Waldorf School, the National Dance Institute, and the New Mexico School for the Arts (formerly the St. Francis Cathedral School). In the warmer months we usually meet at the Harvey Cornell Rose Park (noted for its rose garden) and at Federal Park, the greenest areas one can find in the city with grass and wonderful trees.

During the Covid pandemic, it was difficult to find space to rent, so I continued classes outside even during winters. In Santa Fe, the weather is usually comfortable year round. Even at 38 degrees with blue skies it is fine for taiji outside. Only on windy days would we cancel. What I like best is that the air is dry. It keeps one comfortable even on hot days, without sweating as in humid Pennsylvania. Plus, no mosquitos or flies to disturb practice.

When other martial arts teachers learned I moved to Santa Fe, also known as "The City Different," they thought I'd be overwhelmed by "new age" types. They'd be looking for fantasy taiji rather than the art based in reality. I was warned. Despite some truth in their words and dealing with a few of these fanciful characters, some wonderful students have joined the Winged Lion School of Tai Chi. A few have been studying with me for nearly two decades, including Tom Farrell, Debra Rivera-Sommer, Steve Haines, and William Bruno.

In Santa Fe, I first taught two to four classes per week for some years. With time, the class schedule grew to include ten or more classes per week. I've cut back some now. I stopped teaching at the community collage, but continue at the Pecos Senior Center, a thirty minute drive from Santa Fe, and with a few private classes. Teaching is a joy when the students want to learn and come equipped with patience and good manners. It's not always so. One student with an irritating character can affect the whole class. So, over the years, a number of students were asked to leave. I prefer students feel comfortable as part of a taiji family, practicing together and enjoying the health benefits of the exercise.

Senior student Debra Rivera-Sommer practicing Chen Style cane.

Enter the Novice Student

I've had a good number of people without martial art experience come to my taijiquan class for instruction. I always ask about their background, if they've studied any martial arts or other sports, and why they wished to study. Most have good intentions and also a number of preconceived ideas about taiji. This is true for others seeking instruction in any other martial arts. Please keep this in mind while reading this section to freely replace "taiji" with any other art.

The most bewildering type of individual seeking to study taiji is the one who, without any taiji experience, tells the instructor exactly what they wish to learn. "I want to learn..." How can they tell anyone what they want to learn when they know next to nothing about taiji? I just have to smile and suggest that they find another teacher. Their tea cup is full and no more can be added. Such a student always proves to be difficult in class.

A high-ranking karate black-belt came asking me to teach him and his blackbelt students. He had a caveat. I was to go to his second-floor studio in the evening by a stairway in the back of the building. He didn't want others to know I would be teaching them. Their goal was to quickly learn the fundamental taiji routine in order to teach it and make some additional income. Taiji was becoming popular and he saw an opportunity, but taiji is not a quick study. I turned down the job offer. I wouldn't teach them even if let in the front door.

A young couple had a similar idea. They entered my school and we sat down to discuss why they were interested in taiji. Within two minutes, they asked: "When can we teach?" I replied: You should be asking, "How can we learn?" They too were more interested in making money than learning. They sensed they had entered a school with a different set of values than their own and never returned.

Some longtime martial artists have come to my taiji classes to learn ways to improve their fighting skills. I'm cautious if this is their primary reason to study, especially if they are aggressive types who may have violent tendancies. "I know you can use it. I want to learn techniques and push-hands." One bagua practitioner, who worked as a bouncer, came into my class and the first thing he asked was to push-hands. He wanted to test my skills, but I declined, saying that I only practice push-hands with my students. I have nothing to prove, especially to one only seeking to conquer others and pump up his own ego.

I made a choice early on to teach taiji rather than kuntao knowing that kuntao often attracts aggressive types because it is a very effective fighting art known for its crippling, lethal techniques. I thought that if I taught taiji, most would not be seeking a combat art. If taiji students proved to be good hearted people who later developed an interest self-defense, we would add that aspect into our practice.

Of course most people are drawn to study taiji as an exercise for health. Some see it as a qigong and/or meditative practice. Such students make up the core of practitioners and largely define the art by their influence.

What is taijiquan? A martial art, a wholistic exercise, a dance-like practice, a moving meditation, a competive sport, or something else? Most begin their taiji studies because they are interested in one or two of these facets. Surprisingly, many are unaware that taiji is, or can be, a martial art. Since many practitioners neglect reading about taiji's history, theory and practice, their level of understanding can stagnate. If their teacher is mediocre, the way of progress is further hampered.

The rush to quickly learn movements leads to shallow taiji. In studying the traditional Yang Style long routine in our classes, students learn the movements one at a time. When they can memorize the movement and can perform it fairly well, they move on to the next movement. However, we always review. After getting to the final closing form, one student asked: "What's next? The sword form?" Even with a few years of instruction, she failed to grasp the depth of taiji and the time needed to do it well. She'd forget movements and her movements remained tense, off-balance, and awkward. Learning the movements is only the first step! Then comes the real practice to embody the taiji principles of relaxations and balance. In addition, eventually students should have a basic grasp of applications in the form and the possible variations.

During the earlier years teaching, I wanted to help students learn quickly. I'd give each student a dozen or more corrections to work on. By the end of class they'd only remember one or two of the suggestions made. So, I reduced the number of corrections to five or six. They still would only remember one or two. Now, I give three, with hopes they remember two. A student needs time to think about each correction and practice it over and over so the body and mind remember it. Otherwise, mistakes continue and the taiji form remains sloppy. Polishing takes time and patience is required.

The definition of taiji changes with the deeper understanding that comes over the years. A new student enters the study with their preconceptions and—hopefully with instruction, watching videos, and reading reputable books and articles on the subject—will come to grasp the depths of art. It deepens with time for any serious practitioner.

A teacher has to work with each student, their individual abilities and attitudes. As the student learns, so does the teacher. I've had to learn to adapt to the students' attitudes, ages, and abilities. Are they patient? Do they treat other students with respect? Why do they wish to learn taiji—to teach, show off, or to improve health while learning?

It's a joy to teach students who take their practice seriously while having fun doing it. They can represent the ideals of what good students embody, being attentive, considerate, and dedicated to the learning process. Each taiji student attends classes with their unique mental and physical constitution. Some are disciplined and practice daily while others barely practice while in class. Other factors include age, memory, strength, as well as their individual reasons for learning taiji. Class content continually adjusts for all these reasons.

Giving a speech at the 130th Anniversary in Honor of Grandmaster Xiong Yanghe Yilan city, Taiwan, November 4, 2017. I wrote an article which was published in the commemorative book.

Class of Master Lin Chaolai (on my right), leading representative of the Xiong system today. Another senior is Huang Qinglin, sitting 2nd from right, front row.

The Winged Lion School of Tai Chi

Taijiquan fundamentals are found in the traditional long routine, usually numbered as consisting of 108 movements. I teach a traditional Yang Style as taught by Xiong Yanghe in Taiwan. Practitioners of this system number the long routine at 111 movements. All students work on this and often only this. It can be a lifetime of work. Mainly because of their age, many have a difficult time memorizing all the movements. Those who can memorize the routine then review with greater focus on principles of relaxation, balance, and keeping a slow, even tempo.

One article summed up that learning taiji takes four steps: 1) form 2) feeling 3) functions 4) forgetting. A great percentage of students learn the movements (form) and spend years trying to get the "feeling" of taiji. Few work on functions, such as push-hands and techniques that make up the routine. Rarely do students go beyond this training for real combative skills. "Forgetting" is the ability to move spontaniously with the repertoire of techniques learned over the years.

A good example of learning form and not yet embodying feeling was demonstrated by a lady in a Santa Fe park practicing the long routine with her group. We were practicing in one part of the park and I happened to look over at the other group as a shoe flew about thirty feet in the air. I saw a lady moving slowly according to regular taiji routine practice until coming to the kick, "separate base." Whenever beginners start to loose balance, they usually become more tense and move faster. Because this lady couldn't keep her balance or remain relaxed, she moved quickly to get through the kicking sequence. Thus, the flying shoe.

In Santa Fe, it is easy to see that students in other schools of taiji in town have a limited knowledge of how to use taiji for self-defense. My students were no different. So, I started to teach a basic kuntao form to students just so they could learn how to properly throw a punch. With that, they could move on to learning some of the functions included in the taiji long routine. Learning basic functions improves their forms with hands in proper positions and kicks and pushes on target.

When a student is able to perform the long routine well, embodying the taiji principals, we move on to other practices. Depending on the student, some will learn a basic stick routine or stationary push-hands. More advanced study the straight sword and moving push-hands. Some have studied "dispersing hands" (*sanshou*), a two-person duet. A couple students learned Chen Style's First and Second Routines. My most advanced have learned both sides of sanshou, straight sword, Chen Style Cane, a few kuntao routines, and Hua Tuo's qigong called Five Animal Frolics. Everyone regularly reviews the Yang long routine. Hopefully the other practices help them improve this most fundamental taiji practice.

Below: kuntao taichu practice. Right: Xiong system: *sanshou*, stick, straight sword, broadsword, and 111 solo routine.

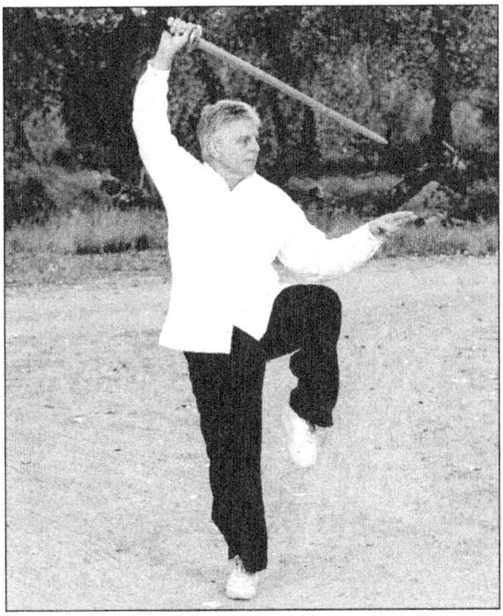
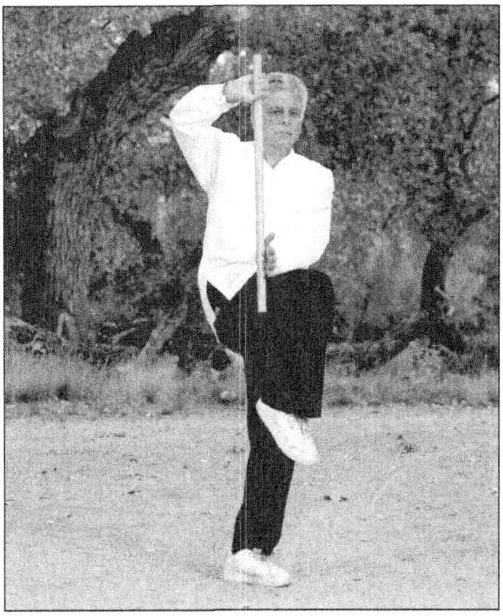
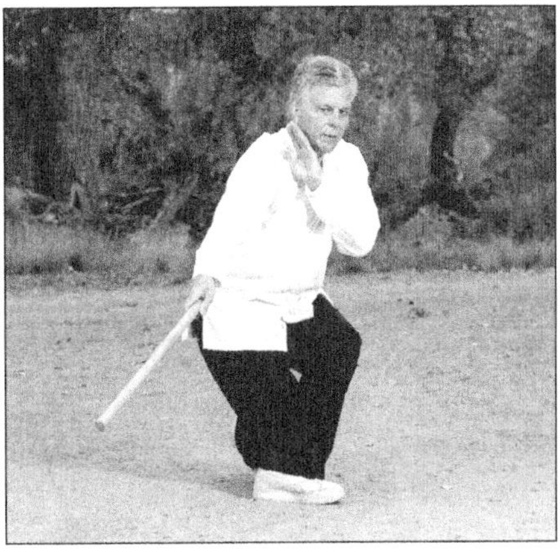
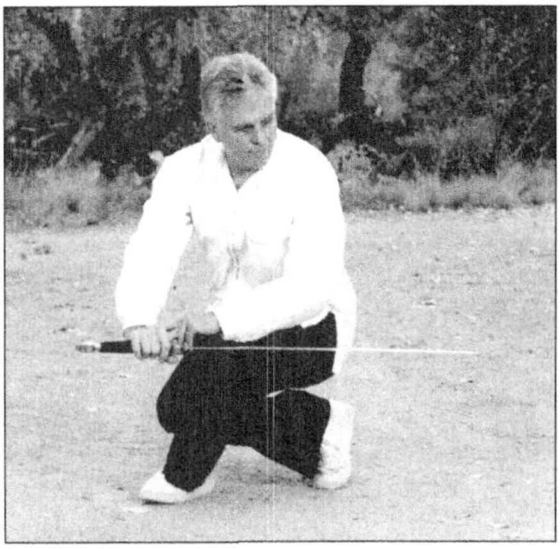
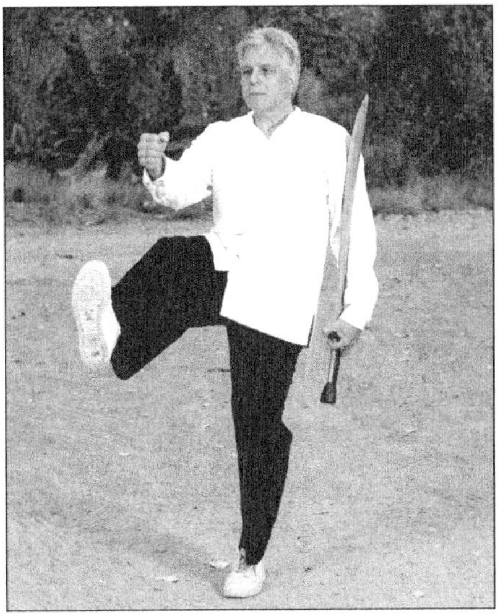
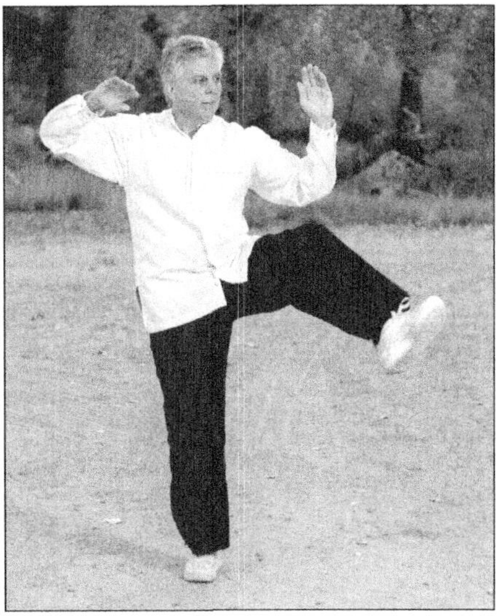

佛光山寺

Fo Guang Shan Monastery,
Kaohsiung, Taiwan,
November 2017.
Photo by Sheng-Hsien Lin.

Postscript

Throughout history, societies have always had to deal with martial arts for their relationship with violence. Real fighting arts have the potential to cripple or kill. Traditionally, there has been some efforts made to instill responsibility and control of fighting skills, including ethical guidelines. Some systems couple martial training with spiritual training for this reason. Today, many of these safeguards are ignored. With the popularity of boxing, especially on television, came social protest to stop the sport as savage violence. Rather than condemn it, masses support it and political and legal leaders turn their heads. It's gotten much worse with the cage events and the popularity of Mixed Martial Arts.

As publisher of the *Journal of Asian Martial Arts* for two decades, it is sad to see how depraved and widespread this activity has become. What people get arrested for occuring in the street, receive millions of dollars as a reward in the cage. Acts of violence should be condemned, but it is allowed only because of the great financial profits some receive. I love the research, study and practice of martial arts, but there is a social responsibility that comes with the learned skills. There is a parallel here with the use of guns.

There is a well known saying encouraging one "To fight the good fight" — to try to make good choices, do the right thing, while encouraging others to do the same. Both individuals and countries turn to using violence for various reasons, including ignorance, greed, profit, fame, or to express power. Violence should be the last resort. Resorting to violence is most often fueled by emotions. Our genes are still infused with survival instincts in a world where the idea of "survival of the fittest" remains dominant.

Going beyond the "good fight," perhaps the best fight would be to work toward adapting martial arts into a civilized lifestyle. It may be a long, long, long road, but we can be optimistic. One or two thousand more years should show some results! Representing this quest, the logo for the *Journal of Asian Martial Arts* was designed with a balance of stylized tips of a sword and pen, the blend of the civil (*wen*) with the martial (*wu*).

General Index

Academie de l'Espee, 80
adapted to modernity, 98-99
aikido, 66-67, 70-71, 73, 77-79, 81-82, 84-86, 88-94, 98-101, 103-105
Ainu, 69, 71
Albuquerque, 14-15, 18, 24-25
Amdur, Ellis, 70-74, 96-97
archery, 50, 73, 83
Aristotelian philosophy, 97
armbar submissions, 100-101
armor, 75
Armstrong, Hunter, 54
Arneil, Steve, 89
Art of War, 68, 100
article submissions, 56-58, 60, 67
asceticism, 93
Attention Deficit/Hyperactivity Disorder, 91-92
auditory elements, 81-82
Autism Spectrum Disorders, 100
axe kick, 91
baguazhang, 19, 42, 78-79, 90, 97, 99, 104, 114
bajiquan, 79-80, 85
Bando, 56, 101-102
bartitsu, 79
Barton-Wright, E. William, 79
Beijing Physical Culture Research Institute, 35
Bernardini, George, 110, 112
Black Belt Magazine, 43, 53
bladed weaponry, 68, 99
Blanks, Billy, 10
Bodhidharma, 67
board breaking, 100-101
body-awareness, 100
body fat, 101-102
Book of Changes (*Yi Jing*), 73, 99
bookstores, 56, 60
breakfalls, 75
breathing, 68, 74, 81, 91
Brinkman, Marcus, 70, 73, 79
British Judo Association, 79-80
Buddhism, 21, 39, 46, 96-97
Buddhist mindfulness, 96-97
bushido, 95

Cao, Delin, 48
Capoeira, 100-101
carotid choke, 97
Carradine, David, 18
Carter, Ed, 25
Chen, Fake, 48, 50
Chen, Mingbiao, 48, 50
Chen Village, 19, 31, 43, 48, 50-51, 83, 88, 90, 95, 103
Chen, Weiming, 37, 75
Chen, Xiaowang, 70, 83, 86
Chen, Xiaoxing, 83
Chen, Yenxi, 43, 48-50
Chenjiagou, see Chen Village
Chinese bronze swords, 100-101
Chinese Gongfu Federation, 13
choke, 89-90, 97, 100-101
chokehold submissions, 100-101
Christiano, Vincent, 8
chum kiu form, 93
Chung Moo, 68
classification, 70-71, 73
Confucius, 14, 33, 66-67, 92, 94
conditioning, 96, 98-99, 104
Cordes, Hiltrud, 23, 30
cowhearding stick, 93
cross-body armlock, 93
crucible steel, 94
Cunningham, Raymond, 4, 9, 18, 25-27
dangerous animals, 28, 98-99
dantian, 100
Daoism, 13, 28, 43, 45, 59, 68-69, 75-76, 80, 93-94, 104
de Thouars, Maurice, 17
de Thouars, Paul, 17, 24, 29
de Thouars, Victor, 17, 24, 29
de Thouars, William, 17, 24, 29
de Vries, Ernest, 17, 20
defending against a blade, 91
distribution, 56-57, 60
Djut, Mas, 17
dojo ritual, 99
Dong Style Taiji, 31, 37
Du, Yuze, 43, 45, 48-51
Durante, Gerald, 8
Dutch, 4, 15-17, 20, 22-25, 56
Dutch East Indies, 15

East 6th and French Street studio, 2, 12
editorial, 55-56, 59, 61, 63-67, 69, 71
Eishin-ryu, 91, 97
Enter the Dragon, 53, 85
Erie, PA, 1-3, 8, 13, 18, 25-27, 106, 109, 111
eskrima, 70, 87-88
European Judo Union, 79-80
fajing, 85
Farrer, Douglas, 23, 30
Feeney, Marilyn, 25
Fife Judo Dojo, 78
Filipino kuntaw, 14, 75-76
First World Congress on Fighting Sports and Martial Arts, 82
Five Animals, 23
Five Animal Frolics, 118
Frost, Brian, 73
Fu, Yonghui, 77
Fu, Zhensong, 73
Fuyru Magazine, 54
Gao, Fangxian, 77-78
Ge, Hong, 94
Geesink, Anton, 20
gender, 92, 98
Geoghegan, Tim, 79
globalization, 95, 100
Goju-ryu, 73-74, 80, 84, 88-89, 93
Goshin Jutsu, 8, 102
ground fighting, 95, 100
Guo, Lianying, 38
hair pin (*taichu, sai,*), 8-12, 14, 16, 27, 30, 71-72, 84-85, 103, 109-110
Han, Qingtang, 73
Hapkido, 81, 91-92, 98-99
head butting, 98
health benefits, 101, 113
Heiki-ryu Jujutsu, 86
Hinduism, 21, 23
Haruna, Matsuo, 73-74
headhunters, 28
Honcho bugei shoden, 70
Hong, Yixiang, 84
Hoplos, 54
Hou, Faxiang, 72
Hsu, Adam, 48
Hu, Puan, 36-37
Hung-Gar, 79

iaido, 68, 70, 91-92, 96-97
Illustrated Manual of Martial Arts (Muye Dobo Tongji), 70-71
immortality, 77
Indonesia, 4, 10, 14-17, 21-25, 27-30, 56, 67, 69, 98-99
injuries, 66, 76, 78, 83
Inside Kung Fu Magazine, 43
integrative combat, 98
Inter-Pacific Tours, 44
internal energy, 100
internal-external schools, 100
International Judo Federation, 79-80
iron ruler, see hair pin
Isshin-ryu, 83
Iwakiri, Ryoichi, 78
Jesus, 96
jodo/jyodo, 66, 75
Johnston, Judith, 110-111
joint locking, 74
Judo Illustrated, 54
jujutsu, 75, 77, 86-89, 104
Kabuki theater, 98
Kano, Jigoro, 9
Kanzaki, Shigekazu, 81
kajukenbo, 69
kalarippayattu, 28, 66, 70-71, 98-99
karate, 3-4, 8-10, 12-13, 19, 24-27, 43, 53, 67-70, 72-79, 81-82, 86, 88, 90, 92-93, 97, 101-104, 114
The Karate Kid, 53
kata, 27, 58, 72, 82, 84-85, 87-94, 97-100, 103-104
Katori Shinto Ryu, 70-71
Kauskas, Jan, 106, 108
kebatinan, 70
kendo, 84-85, 95
Kharbarelli pick-up, 94-95
Khun Khmer Boran, 89-90
kickboxing, 82, 84-85
Kim, Richard, 91
Kinjo, Hiroshi, 70
knife, 40, 46, 70-71, 109
kobudo, 71, 78-79, 84, 104
Kodokan judo, 25, 94, 98, 102
Kokusai Budoin, 71
Koshin-ryu, 83

Krishnamurti, Jiddu, 89-90
kumite strategies, 81
kuntao, 1, 14, 21-22, 30, 80-81, 98-99, 106, 108-109, 111, 114, 118
kuntao-silat, 23-24, 26-29, 98
Kurosaka/Tentoku Kan Dojo, 76
Kwong, Wing Lam, 82, 95
Kyokushin, 75-76, 89-90
Kyu Sun-Hui, 91
kyudo, 66
Larense Garrote, 86
law enforcement, 63, 70-71
Le, Huanzhi, 37, 41
Lee, Bruce, 4, 8, 18, 85, 89-90
Lee, Houchen, 48
leg lock, 90
Leth Wei, 89-90
Li Family taijiquan, 89
liability, 83-85
Liang, Dongcai, 38
Lin, Chaolai, 41
Lin, Jianhong, 41, 96-97
lion dancing, 91
Liu, Xiheng, 98
Lo, Benjamin Pang Jeng, 74
Lo, Dexiu, 70
Lopez, Richard, 4, 8-13, 18, 20, 25-27, 29, 106, 109, 112
Lore, James, 91
lower spinal rotation, 89
Lu, Jia, 88
Maiden of Yue, 93-94
makiwara, 68, 98-99
Maniwa Nen-ryu, 72
Mark, Gin-foon, 68
marketing, 86-87
martial-acrobatic arts, 82
martial art movies, 53, 66, 77-78, 84-85, 104
Martial Arts: The Real Story, 82
martial dance, 23, 28, 84-85
martial music, 28, 84-85, 88
Masaryk University, 102
massage therapies, 71-72
masterless warriors, 88
maximizing speed, 100
McKissick, Reginald, 106, 108
Meibukan Gojyu Ryu, 93

Minowa, Katsuhiko, 78
Miyagi, Chojun, 70, 73
Miyamoto, Musashi, 79-80
Mixed Martial Arts, 86, 89, 98, 103, 121
Modern Arnis, 93
Mongolian wrestling, 85
Moren, Juan, 91
Morgan, Andrè, 84-85
Motobu-ryu, 74
mounted archery, 73
Mu Dong Martial Arts School, 13
Muay Thai, 86
multiple intelligences, 100
Murakami, Katsumi, 79, 95
Muromoto, Wayne, 54
Muso Jikiden Eishin-ryu Iaido, 91
Mystic Origins of the Martial Arts, 78
mysticism, 23, 28, 69-70, 103
naginata, 71-72
Nahate, 100
Nakhom Pathom, 17
nationalism, 71, 95
Netherlands, 15, 20
Nihonto, 101
Ninjitsu, 74
ninpo, 73-74
nutrition, 84, 104
observational learning, 86, 90
Okano, Isao, 87
Okinawa, 4, 53, 67, 71-72, 74, 77, 83-86, 88, 100, 104
Omori-ryu, 85
O'Neill, Dermot M., 86
oral traditions, 77
orange sash, 3, 10, 26
Oyama, Mas, 75
Parker, Dexter, 106, 108
parry, 95
patterns, 2, 72, 87-88, 99, 102
pauleh tinggi ceremony, 30, 72
228 Peace Memorial Park, 32
Pecos Senior Center, 113
pencak silat, 22-23, 29, 72
penitentiary defense, 98, 101-102
Pepperman, Thomas, 1-3, 5-9, 26-27, 106
performance, 72, 79, 101-102
personality, 33, 35, 49, 88-89

physical exercise, 19, 32, 38, 40, 63, 74, 93, 104, 113, 115
physique, 101-102
piguazhang, 79
pineal gland, 98
Polish martial arts, 94, 96
politics, 21, 65, 73-74, 93, 104
praying mantis, 75, 81, 83
Presas, Remy, 92-93
pressure points (*dianxue*), 83, 91-92
profit, 54, 64, 73-74, 104, 121
progressive instruction, 96
Pukulan, 17, 20, 28
Puli city, 43, 46
push-hands (*tuishou*), 32, 41, 93, 100, 114, 117-118
Pwang Gai Noon Ryu, 68-69
Pythian Temple, 3, 7-9
qigong, 40, 68, 72, 77, 101-103, 115, 118
Qingping straight sword, 96-97
Randai folk theatre, 23, 30, 75, 85
Ratti, Oscar, 62, 82, 105, 108
red sash, 7-8
Reeders, Cornelis, 15, 17
Reeders, Theo, 15, 17
Reeders, Willem, 2-4, 6-10, 12-21, 24-27, 29, 98, 106, 109, 111
regulation, 77
Renkoho, 95
rhythm, 88, 102
Ricci, Brian, 91
right to bear arms, 101
risk society, 91-92
Rivera-Sommer, Debra, 113
romanization, 3, 14, 59, 63
ryuha system, 70, 72
Rosenfeld, Arthur, 97
Royal Kung Fu, 3-4, 8, 13, 15
sai, see hair pin
Saito, Mark, 74
Saito ninjitsu, 74
Sakugawa Koshiki Shorinji-ryu, 77
sambo, 74, 79-80, 95, 104
samurai, 58, 72, 79-80, 90, 105, 108
Sanseru, 83
sanshou (dispersing hands), 32, 38, 40, 93, 118
Santa Fe, NM, 112-113, 117

Savelli, Guy, 4
scabbards, 81
Sealy, Ed, 25
self-defense, 1, 63, 65, 71, 102, 110-111, 115, 117
self-transformation, 78, 80
Seong, Liu, 15-17, 19, 25, 106, 108
Serak, 22, 29
Servidio, Robert, 12, 25
Seton Hall University, 43, 107
Shanghai, 36, 44, 75-76
Shaolin staff, 88
Shaolin Temple, 16, 20, 31, 77
Sheldon, Patrick, 4
Shi, Diaome, 38
Shibata, Kanjuro, 82-83
Shintani, Masaru, 92
Shishochin, 83
shoulder wheel throw, 88
Shorinjin-ryu, 74
Shotokan karate, 25, 70
shoulder throw, 88, 96-97
shuaijiao, 91-92
sil lum tao, 72
silat, 1, 14-15, 18-19, 21-30, 56, 69-70, 72, 76, 85, 87, 98-99
Silat Seni Gayong, 69
Silek, 30, 75
Silk Route, 95
Simmons, Artis, 10
single palm change, 78
Sinmoo Hapkido, 91, 98-99
skin infections, 97
sling, 84-85, 103
Smith, Robert W., 30, 54, 61, 71-75, 77-79-80, 82-83, 105, 108
Sohei, 68
spear, 40, 50, 92-93, 96, 103
spirit boxing, 79-80
sport, 28-29, 53-54, 63-64, 70, 78, 82, 86, 98-99, 102, 114-115, 121
staff, 9, 40, 70-71, 86, 88, 93
stillness, 74
stomach armlock, 88
Stone, Michael, 107-108
student-instructor, 82
studio (Lopez), 10, 11-12, 109-110, 112

studio (French St.), 2
studio (Cunningham), 9, 11-12, 18, 26
submission holds, 74
Sugawara, Tetsutaka, 86
sumo, 79, 101-102
Sun, Lutang, 37
Sun Family Taiji, 95, 104
Surabaya, 15
sword, 9, 32, 40, 66, 68-69, 71, 73-75, 80, 83, 85-86, 88, 91, 95-97, 99-104, 108-111, 115, 118, 121
sword-cutting practice, 101
sword tracings (*oshigata*), 100
Sykes, Arthur, 1-9, 18, 25-27, 29, 106
Systema, 88, 95, 104
taekwondo, 59, 66-67, 75-76, 78, 85, 87, 91, 93, 98-103
taekyon, 68, 70, 104
Taft Museum, 69, 74
taichu, see hair pin
taiji ruler, 94
taijiquan, 19, 31, 35-38, 40, 48-51, 59, 66-79, 83-86, 88-90, 92-95, 97-102, 106, 109, 114-115, 117
Taipei, 31-32, 43, 45, 51, 84
Takashi, Kinjo, 77
talent detection, 98-99
tameshigiri, 101
tameshiwari, 73-74
Tamura, Masato, 78
Tamura, Vince, 86
Tanemura, Shoto, 73
teaching the Deaf, 88-89
Teenage Mutant Ninja Turtles, 55
tensegrity, 98
Tensho kata, 82
Than Quyen, 88
Thang-ta, 77-78
Thibault, Gerard, 80
Thumma, Betty, 110
Thunderdome, 84-85
Tibetan Taichi, 19
timing, 102
To-on-ryu, 81
tournaments, 2-6, 8, 12-13, 16, 18, 20, 27, 53, 55
training the lower body, 98-99
Tsuruoka, Masami, 86

Tu, Zongren, 43-46, 48-49
Uehara, Seikichi, 74
Uechi-ryu, 93
Ueshiba, Morihei, 86
ukiyo-e, 79
Ultimate Fighting Championships, 100-101
Via Media Publishing, 53, 56-57, 61, 65, 105, 109
Ving Tsun, see Wing Chun
violence, 63-64, 71-72, 85, 104, 121
visualization, 94
Vivekananda College, 12
Waboku Jujutsu, 77
walking stick, 90, 103
Wang, Xian, 84
warming-up, 73
watered steel, 93
Watts riots, 6
website, 56, 60
Webster-Doyle, Terrance, 75, 86
weight training, 73-74
Werbrouck, Ulla, 85
Westbrook, Adele, 62, 105, 108
Wetzel, Willy, 24
White Ape Tongbei, 87, 89
White Crane, 23
Wieling, Christina, 15
Wilson, Don, 82
Wing Chun/Ving Tsun, 72, 93, 100-101, 104
Winged Lion School of Tai Chi, 112-113, 117
women, 73-74, 98, 100, 104
Wong, Curtis, 81
Wong, Sam, 13, 20
wooden replica weapons, 86-87
World Martial Arts Hall of Fame, 69
World War II, 22, 34, 95
Wu, Chao-xiang, 91
Wu, Daxin, 91
Wu, Jianquan, 37
Wu, Kuang-hsien, 66
wushu, 68, 77-78, 100-101
Xiong Style Taiji, 36, 38, 40-41, 96-97
Xiong Yanghe 130th Anniversary, 47
xia tradition, 100-101, 107-108
xingyi, 59, 70-71, 83-85, 90-92, 97, 104

Xiong, Yanghe, 35-41
Yabu, Kentsu, 82
yabusame, 72
Yagi, Meitatsu, 88, 93
Yamada, Yoshimitsu, 90
Yang, Banhou, 35
Yang, Chengfu, 35, 37-38
Yang, Jianhou, 35, 37-38
Yang, Jwing-ming, 86
Yang, Luchan, 35
Yang, Shaohou, 35, 37
Yang, Yang, 81
Yang, Qingyu, 31-34, 41-42, 45
Yilan city, 38-39, 116
yoga, 70, 101
Yue, Fei, 91
Zhang, Songxi, 100
Zheng, Manqing, 38, 69, 71-75, 95, 106
Zhou, Harrold, 31
Zimmerman, Harry, 25
zurkhaneh, 87, 89

Author Index
published in the
Journal of Asian Martial Arts
Number in brackets [#] indicates the number of articles published

Acevedo, William [1], 98
Adrogué, Manuel [1], 86-87
Alamudeen, Saleen [1], 94-95
Allan, David [2], 84-85
Amdur, Ellis [4], 70-74, 96-97
Amos, Daniel [1], 79-80
Anderson, Scott [1], 79-80
Anta, Julio [1], 96
Asmundson, Gordon [1], 62
Babin, Richard [1], 81
Baek, Bosco Seung-Chul [1], 100
Bailey, Thomas [1], 97
Baldwin, Fred [1], 69, 71
Barlow, Jeffrey [1], 69
Barnet, Jay [1], 86
Barnfield, Anne [2], 86-89
Bates, Christopher [1], 68
Behrendt, James [1], 83
Bercades, Luigi [1], 91
Berwick, Stephan [4], 83, 86, 91, 96
Bialokur, Nicolae [1], 94-95
Binder, Brad [1], 77
Bluming, Jon [1], 77-78, 82
Bolelli, Daniele [2], 86, 89
Bolz, Mary [4], 68, 71-72, 77, 84
Boudreau, Françoise [1], 72
Bowen, Richard [1], 79-80
Bradley, Sean [2], 91, 98
Breslow, Arieh [1], 77
Brinkman, Marcus [2], 70, 73, 79
Brodsky, Greg [1], 101
Brooks, Lisa [1], 79
Brown, S. Dale [1], 100
Brown, Steven C. [1], 86
Bryant, Andrew [1], 97
Burdick, Dakin [2], 59, 75-76, 87, 89
Burroughs, Jake [2], 95, 98
Butler, Dannie [1], 86
Cai, Naibiao [1], 91
Câmara, Fernando [1], 93
Campbell, Perry, 90
Carleton, Nicholas [1], 92
Cartmell, Tim [1], 97
Chaudhuri, Joyotpaul [2], 72, 93
Cheung, Donald [1], 93
Cheung, Mei [1], 98
Clark, Strider [1], 87-89
Cohen, Kenneth [1], 94
Coleman, Donald [1], 77
Cook, Morgan [1], 79
Cooper, Eric [2], 90-92
Cordes, Ars [1], 84
Craig, Kevin [1], 79
Crawford, Andrew [1], 67
Crider, Duane [1], 101
Cruicchi, Bruno [1], 86
Cynarski, Wojciechv, 94, 97
Czarnecka, Marzena [1], 82
Dalia, Albert [1], 100-101
Daneshgar, Shahyar [1], 87
Davies, Philip H.J. [1], 80
Davis, Barbara [1], 73-74
Davis, Donald [1], 74
Davison, Phil, 100-101
Davey, Hugh [2], 71, 73
Day, Morgan [1], 69
Della Pia, John [2], 70-71

Delza, Sophia [1], 67
DeMarco, Michael [16], 66, 68, 70, 74-75, 77, 80, 85-86, 88, 96, 98, 108
DeRose, Dayn [1], 74
DeRose, John Richard [1], 87
Derrickson, Carol [1], 68
DiCristofano, Anthony [1], 100-101
Dohrenwend, Robert [5], 84-85, 90, 92-93, 98-99, 103
Dong, Xunyin, 96
Donohue, John [12], 66, 68-71, 75, 81-82, 84-86, 89-92
Dowd, Steven [1], 75
Drape, Steven [1], 86-87
Drengson, Alan [1], 66
Durstine, Larry [1], 73
Dykhuizen, C. Jeffrey, [2], 81, 86
Ebell, S. Biron [1], 94
Edinborough, Campbell [1], 99
Edwards, Dwight [1], 81
Eisen, Martin [1], 68
Emerick, Danny [1], 98
Espartero, Julián [1], 87, 89
Espinosa, Avelina [4], 84, 88, 91
Ferguson, Rhadi [2], 100-101
Figler, Robert [4], 79-80, 85, 88
Filipiak, Kai [1], 98-99
Finch, David [6], 83, 85, 87-88, 91
Flanagan, Sean [1], 80
Florence, Richard [5], 71-72, 74-75, 83, 91
Folman, Ralph [1], 72
Freund, Ronald [1], 73
Friday, Karl [1], 72-73
Friman, H. Richard [4], 73, 77, 79-80
Fu, Brian [1], 85
Gaffney, David [3], 88, 90, 95
Galas, Matthew [1], 75
Gatling, Lance [2], 94, 102
Gauthier, Maurice [1], 98
Gilbey, John [1], 86
Goedecke, Christopher [1], 83
Goedkoop, James [1], 86-87
Golden, Bryan [1], 89-90
Gong, Henry [1], 89
Gourley, Bernard [1], 89
Graebner, Peter [1], 90
Grady, James [2], 77-78, 81-82

Graycar, Michael Rosario [1], 98
Greer, John Michael [1], 80
Grossman, Eliot Lee [2], 77, 91
Gutiérrez, Carlos [2], 87, 89, 98
Hackney, Charles [1], 97
Hallam, Jeffrey [1], 83
Hanon, Michael [1], 98
Harrison-Pepper, Sally [1], 68
Hawthoren, Mark [1], 80
Hayduk, Dina [1], 101
Heijmans, John [2], 85, 93
Hendrey, Elisa [1], 75
Henning, Stanley [15], 75, 77, 79-80, 83, 88, 90-95, 100, 104
Hershey, Lewis [1], 70
Hesselink, Reinier [1], 72-73
Hlinak, Matt [1], 96-97
Hobart, Peter [7], 91-93, 95-97, 101
Holcombe, Charles [2], 67-69
Holt, Ronald [1], 73
Hopkins, Giles [5], 85, 87, 89, 93, 97
Hoshino, Harunaka [1], 68
Hoyt, Stephen [1], 71
Hsu, Chris [1], 96
Hurst, G. Cameron [2], 69, 72-73
Imamura, Hiroyuki [1], 67
Jacques, Brett [1], 79-80
Jensen, Mark [1], 82
Jeremiah, Ken [1], 93-94
Jirgensons, Dainis [1], 77
Joern, Travis [1], 99
Jones, Brian [1], 97
Jones, David [1], 66
Jones, Llyr [3], 90, 98, 102
Kachur, Shane [1], 92
Kauz, Herman [1], 93
Kelland, Mark [1], 96-97
Kemerly, Tony [1], 83
Kennedy, George [1], 90
Khorasani, Manouchehr [2], 93-94
Kinzey, Stephen [1], 83
Klens-Bigman, Deborah [4], 79, 82-83, 88, 98
Ko, Yong Jae [2], 86, 95
Koepfer, Stephen [1], 95
Kohler, Stuart [2], 71, 78
Konzak, Burt [1], 72
Labbate, Marvin [5], 79-80, 82, 84, 99

Lajcik, Timothy [1], 94
Lam, Wing [1], 94
Lang, Tom [1], 94
Laurent, Douglas [1], 67
Lehrhaupt, Linda [1], 68-69
Levitas, Alex [1], 80
Levitt, Ellen [1], 73
Lianto, Andy [2], 85, 88
Lim, Peter Lim Tian Tek [2], 71, 74
Linden, Paul [1], 100
Lo, Benjamin [1], 98
Lohse, Frederick [1], 78, 80
Long, Joe [1], 75
Loong, Loh Han [1], 100
Looser, Diana [1], 91-92
Loupos, John [1], 88
Lorden, Michael [1], 75
Lowry, David [1], 88
Macaraeg, Ruel [2], 96, 99
Magnuson, Jon [1], 69
Mainfort, Donald [1], 77
Maliszewski, Michael [6], 66-67, 81-82, 84
Mallon, Scott [1], 89-90
Mancuso, Ted, [2] 74, 81
Mann, Lawrence [1], 74
Manyak, Anne [1], 67
Mark, Duncan [1], 81
Masciotra, Domenic [1], 85
Mason, Russ [3], 82-83, 95, 98
Massey, Patrick [1], 68
Bild, Matt [1], 90
McCabe, Jack [2], 70, 73
McCarthy, Patrick [1], 70
McCullough, Peter [1], 98
McCurry, John [1], 91
McKenna, Mario [7], 78-79, 81, 93, 100
Miller-Lane, Jonathan [1], 92-93
Moenig, Udo [1], 99
Mok, Olivia [1], 83
Monday, Nyle [1], 70
Monzon, Manuel [1], 85
Mosher, Hal [1], 100
Mukhopadhyay, Bandana [1], 84-85
Murakami, Katsumi [1], 95
Nakazawa, Anthony [1], 67
Neide, Joan [4], 71, 78, 95, 98
Nemeth, David [1], 67

Netherton, Brett [1], 73
Ng, Wai-Ming [1], 73
Niiler, Timothy [3], 77-78, 89, 98
Nix, Charles [1], 83
Noble, Graham [2], 79, 89
Nongmaithem, Khilton [1], 77
Nunberg, Noah [2], 83-85
Nurchis, Roberto [1], 84
O'Connor, Miriam [1], 77
Oga-Baldwin, Quint [1], 95
Ohmi, Goyo [1], 73, 75
Olson, Gregory [1], 79, 85
Ondash, Allan [1], 79
O'Regan, David [1], 89-90
Ouyang, Young [1], 75
Overill, Richard [1], 96
Parker, Chris [1], 72
Parker, Patrick [1], 82-83
Patterson, William [1], 95
Pauka, Kirstin [4], 72, 75-76, 85
Paul, Josh, 100
Paz-y-Miño, Guillermo [6], 81, 84, 88, 91
Peck, Andy [1], 79
Pegg, Richard [3], 68, 83, 100-101
Peritz, Curt [1], 69, 71
Phelps, Shannon [3], 73-74, 77
Pieter, Willy [11], 66, 68-69-70, 76, 78, 85, 91, 93, 98-99, 101-102
Pittman, Allen [6], 75-76, 78-79, 96, 98-99
Polland, Rick [2], 70-71, 75
Polyakov, Leonid [1], 74
Porta, John [2], 70, 73
Profatilov, Ilya [1], 83
Ralston, Peter [1], 82
Rhoads, C.J. [1], 101
Ròman, Francisco [2], 98, 101
Rosenberg, Daniel [1], 71
Rowe, Marc [1], 97
Roxborough, Shannon [1], 100
Rymaruk, Ihor [1], 93
Saporta, José [1], 91
Savage, Martin [1], 102
Schneider, Sara [1], 98
Scott, Steve [1], 93-94
Seckler, Jonathan [1], 66
Secours, Kevin [2], 88, 95

Seidman, Yaron [1], 83
Sheetz-Runkle, Becky [1], 100
Sheridan, Brian [1], 96
Shine, Jerry [2], 68, 70
Sieg, Brandon [1], 75-76
Silvan, Jim [2], 67, 77
Simpkins, Annellen [1], 92
Simpkins, C. Alexander [1], 92, 94
Skaggs, Jeremy [1], 86
Smith, James [1], 90
Smith, Paul [1], 98
Smith, Robert W. [9], 71-75, 77, 79, 108
Soderholm, Maija [1], 87
Spiessbach, Michael [1], 67
Stebbins, John [2], 68-69
Stein, Joel [2], 68, 84
Stubenbaum, Dietmar, [3], 66, 70
Suenaka, Roy [2], 77, 99
Suino, Nicklaus [2], 70, 91
Sun, Makai [1], 79
Sutton, Nigel [2], 68-69
Symmes, Edwin [1], 98
Svinth, Joseph [5], 76, 78-79, 82, 84
Taaffe, Dennis [1], 66
Taylor, Chad [1], 99
Taylor, John [1], 73
Taylor, Kimberly [7], 68, 70, 73, 75, 82, 96
Tedeschi, Marc [1], 81
Tharp, Andrew [1], 101
Tomlinson, Rachel [1], 98
Toth, Olga [1], 86
Toth, Robert [7], 83-84, 86, 88, 91-93
Tran, Jason [1], 88
Tyrey, Bradford [1], 73
Van Horne, Wayne [2], 74, 77
Van Rheenen, Derek [1], 100
Van Ryssegem, Guido [1], 76
Varley, Paul [1], 72-73
Vey, Gregory [1], 98
Vlad, I. [1], 94-95
Vogel, Richard, 90
Wada, Suien [1], 95
Wallace, Adam [1], 77
Ward, Bob [1], 78
Ward, Peter [1], 101
Watson, Christopher [2], 73, 77
Webb, James [1], 86
Webb, Jeff [3], 93, 96, 100

Webster-Doyle, Terrence [1], 86
Wedlake, Lee [1], 97
Wells, Marnix [1], 100
Wile, Douglas [1], 93-94
Wiley, Mark [6], 69-70, 72-73, 75
Willmont, Dennis [1], 75-76
Wilson, James [1], 68-69
Winborne, Duvon [1], 101
Wingard, Geoffrey [3], 84-86, 96-97
Wingate, Carrie [1], 68
Wolfe, Robert [4], 72, 75-76, 79, 95
Wolfson, Greg [1], 93
Wolske, Justin [1], 87
Wong, Jiaxiong [1], 66
Wong, Yuenming [1], 89
Xu, Yizhong [1], 98
Xu, Zhengmei [1], 98
Yang, Jin Bang [1], 95
Yang, Nicholas [1], 99
Yang, Tony [4], 79-80, 85, 88
Yankauskas, Ionas [1], 74
Yao, Haishing [1], 82
Yiannakis, Linda [2], 100, 102
Yokoyama, Kazumasa [1], 70
Yoshinaga, Sakuyama [1], 81
Young, Robert [1], 68
Young, Will Robin [1], 91
Yu, Robert Lin-yi [2], 83-84
Yuan, Weiming [1], 98
Zarrilli, Phillip [4], 66, 70-71
Zerling, Andrew [4], 89-90, 101
Zhang, Yun [2], 87, 91
Zheng, Shuai [1], 100

Printed in Great Britain
by Amazon